"Will I be on television?"

"Thank you for writing a beautiful and uplifting story. I admire your perseverance in the face of rejection. Your love and commitment to your daughter and family outweighs the enormous odds that were against you. "Will I Be on Television?" is a must read for all families of children with special needs. Quite frankly, it should be a must read for everyone – to help broaden our understanding.
Jim Landry

"I loved your book. I devoured it and could not put it down. The writing was wonderful and I couldn't wait to turn the pages.
Joanie Robertson

"There are few books about special needs. They are vague or clinical. Yours is a real help."
The mother of a child with special needs

"Once I started, I couldn't put it down."
Edie Canon

I cannot put into words how wonderful your book was. It is a beautiful story and so well written, I know it came from your heart. This is a book that should be a Number One best seller. There are many people who would have given up. But the love and affection that you, your daughter and son gave this girl is a great story about a family that would not give up."
Allison Esposito

"You have taken a life experience and turned it into a monument to the human spirit, to inspire others, to give them hope as they make their own way through these challenges. It is inspirational for those who don't have special needs children.
Mollie Miller

"I am nominating you for the Pulitzer award. I'm truly overwhelmed. Your book will help 1000's."
Henrietta, Countess de Hoernle

"Will I be on television?"

A Special Needs Child Who Wouldn't Give Up

Jan Amis Jessup

with Susan E. Folstein, M.D.

TATE PUBLISHING
AND ENTERPRISES, LLC

Will I Be on Television?
Copyright © 2014 by Jan Amis Jessup. All rights reserved.

No part of this publication may be reproduced, stored in a retrieval system or transmitted in any way by any means, electronic, mechanical, photocopy, recording or otherwise without the prior permission of the author except as provided by USA copyright law.

This book is designed to provide accurate and authoritative information with regard to the subject matter covered. This information is given with the understanding that neither the author, the collaborator, nor Tate Publishing, LLC is engaged in rendering legal, or professional advice. Since the details of your situation are fact dependent, you should additionally seek the services of a competent professional. The author, collaborator, and publisher specifically disclaim any liability, loss or risk, personal or otherwise, which is incurred as a consequence, directly or indirectly, of the use and application of any of the contents of this book.

The opinions expressed by the author are not necessarily those of Tate Publishing, LLC.

Published by Tate Publishing & Enterprises, LLC
127 E. Trade Center Terrace | Mustang, Oklahoma 73064 USA
1.888.361.9473 | www.tatepublishing.com

Tate Publishing is committed to excellence in the publishing industry. The company reflects the philosophy established by the founders, based on Psalm 68:11,
"The Lord gave the word and great was the company of those who published it."

Book design copyright © 2014 by Tate Publishing, LLC. All rights reserved.
Cover design by Allen Jomoc
Interior design by Jomar Ouano

Published in the United States of America

ISBN: 978-1-63122-081-4
1. Biography & Autobiography / Personal Memoirs
2. Biography & Autobiography / Medical
14.08.18

This book is dedicated to my daughters and
the dear friend who was the first to understand that
Lindsay was a gift from God.

To My Beloved Daughters

Lindsay, Our Star

Cary, My Best Friend

and

In Loving Memory

of

Betty Amis Pond

Acknowledgments

My heartfelt gratitude to all the dear and generous angels who have shared their knowledge, experience, instruction and their constant support throughout the years of my research and writing this book. To those listed here and to the many others, too numerous to mention. I hope you know how sincerely you are appreciated.

Susan E. Folstein, M.D. my dedicated confidant and collaborator, whose help and caring for others knows no boundaries.

Cary Gorsline
Jack Meiners
Michele Holtfreter
Mollie and Ambassador David Miller
Margot and Herschell Gordon Lewis
Mari Messer
Leslie Raemdonck
Roxy Heyse
The Forum on Women's Health
The Bible Study Group
Dearest Mo Miller
Jane Kluczkowski
Jane Malfitano
Charles B. Nemeroff, M.D.
Carolyn Shimkus
Craig and Nancy Johnson
Diane Pacelli
William Jessup

Rosemary Auclair
Nancy Toomey
Dorothy Bedford
Paul Sallarulo
Dr. Sherry Kelly
Michele Rubin

'My special thank you' to everyone at Tate who has worked with me.

Katja Tysdal
Rachael Sweeden
Tosha Powel
Chris Coffey
Travis King
Samuel Bello
and many others

Cover Designed by Allen Jomoc

Contents

Foreword 11

A Terrifying Discovery 13
We Didn't Know What We Didn't Know 23
A Shattering Diagnosis 31
"There Are Institutions" 39
"It Didn't Come From Our Side of the Family" 49
"Dogs Can Walk, Too" 59
"Y...Because We Like You" 67
"They Pushed Me" 75
"Where is Daddy?" 85
"Grass Soup" 93
"I'm One of the Girls" 103
"City of Angels" 111
"Whatever Puts a Sparkle in a Child's Eyes" 119
"Of Course I'm an Angel" 127
"I Felt Terrible. I was Scared. I was Petrified." 139
"My Name is Lins" 149
"I Got Lost in the Chicago Airport" 159
A Decision Dilemma 167
"They Called Me Retard" 177

"I'm a Girl Scout" 185
"I Want to Make My Own Decisions" 195
"We Learned to Love our New Family" 203
"I'm Employee of the Month" 211
"Did You Know Lindsay Has a Heart Murmur?" 219
"Cary, I'm in Trouble" 227
"Surprise Me" 235
A Journey of Experience, Education and Enlightenment 247

Afterword 257

Foreword

Your child is born on Easter Sunday.

Professionals, members of your own family, tell you—in so many words—"she's worthless"

But she's an adorable toddler. She's independent. She's courageous. She meets challenges head-on.

Her siblings love her and learn from living with her. She plans her own birthday parties to the last T, then tells you, "I want it to be a
SURPRISE PARTY!
She's a perfect example of the Dr. Seuss quote,

*"A Person is a Person, no matter how small.
A Person is a Person, after all."*

and

You are an investigative journalism grad and a social worker. How could you *NOT* share her story and your research of *HELP*, resources and *HOPE* along the way, with other parents and families in similar situations?

and

Oh Yes!
Each day she calls you and asks,
"Are you working on my book?" (as,*"Get on with it!)* then,
"Will I be on Television?"

Life—What you get out of it depends on how you play it. Whether you think you can or think you can't, you're absolutely right.

—Anonymous

A Terrifying Discovery

The night before our contented lives turned upside down, I was relaxing with a book on our living room couch. Across the room my husband, Don, was laughing and adding his dramatics to a bedtime story for Cary, our three-year-old daughter. With his tie off and sleeves rolled to his elbows Don lay back in his favorite armchair, roomy enough for a person and a half. We'd labeled it the 'Big Daddy' chair. On his lap, Cary snuggled ever deeper into his arms as he embellished his story with funny faces and silly accents.

His feet were stretched in front of him on the ottoman. Every few minutes he'd wiggle his toes. Our intrigued child giggled with delight at each wiggle. In yellow pajamas, fragrant from her bath she cuddled in his arms. With her little girl lisp she picked out words to repeat as her Daddy read her favorite Dr. Suess's nonsense tale, *Horton Hears a Who!* "One day, on the fifteenth of May in the jungle of Nool, Horton, the elephant, meets the microscopic inhabitants of Whoville."

"A person's a person no matter how small," Don read. "Person, small," Cary's wee voice mimicked him as she pointed to a picture in the book. I watched the two of them from across the living room, captivated and careful not to interrupt.

I would always remember the happiness of those few moments. The image of our innocent family scene is unforgettable. Had I the gift of foresight, I would have treasured that time even more. Nothing like it would ever happen again.

"Did you hear the baby cry?" Don turned to me, breaking my reverie.

"No," I said. I didn't hear a sound from the baby. I wasn't surprised that I might not hear Lindsay. She was four-and-a-half months old, but she didn't have a loud cry. She was a quieter baby than Cary had been. Getting up from the couch, I started toward the nursery. "I'll look in on her," I said over my shoulder.

In Minneapolis late summer and early fall weather can be unpredictable. Some days will be bathed in the warmth of Indian Summer. Shirts come off. Convertible tops go down. At other times, cold winds and rain are harbingers of the long winter to follow. Unpredictably, that night a cold wind was picking up. The summer of 1953 was rapidly turning into fall.

As I walked quickly to Lindsay's room, I could hear the rattle of a loose shutter outside a dining room window. I'll remember to ask Don to fasten it, I thought. The night wind had become stronger since I'd put our baby to bed.

Nearer to the nursery, I heard Lindsay clearly. Her usual soft cry had turned into a much louder explosion of frustration. Ordinarily, she was placid, an easy baby. A tiny girl with a baby's button nose, she had blue eyes and brown hair as soft as corn silk.

As I came into the room I recognized the problem immediately. A rush of cold air was coming from a half-opened window. Lindsay was on her back in her infant crib, clutching the corner of her woolly pink blanket in a tiny fist. Most of the coverlet was heaped haphazardly where she'd kicked it away. With her nightie bunched around her waist above her diaper, she was uncovered, cold and miserable. As hard as she could she pumped her little legs. One pink bootie was off. Her eyes streamed tears.

I shut the window, scooped her up, blanket and all, and held her close to my body's heat. She squirmed. She didn't stop fretting. I cuddled and rocked her, trying to soothe her and circling the small nursery with her in my arms. At times she'd stop fussing for a minute or two and look up at me. Then her cries began again.

Briefly, she'd respond to my "mommy's here" or "see your teddy bear" or descriptions of the puppies and kittens I'd painted on the nursery's pink walls. Then her fretting returned as if it had never stopped. I rocked and stroked her tiny body through the blanket for a long time, until I could tell she was no longer cold.

With her diaper and gown changed, perfumed with baby powder and in a warmer and more comfortable nursery, I was sure she'd settle down. But each time I tried to put Lindsay back into her crib, her crying, fretfulness and squirming began again.

Eliminating possibilities like teething because she was too young, I wondered if she'd been chilled more than I realized and was catching a cold. It was hard to tell. Her temperature wasn't elevated. Her breathing seemed normal. Her tiny nose wasn't runny or stuffy.

Distractions might soothe her, I thought. I carried her to the living room. Don was just closing the story book. I heard him say to Cary, "time to go to bed."

"One more story, please?" Cary wheedled. Her question always made us laugh. It was our three-year-old's beginning of a nightly routine to delay bedtime. Don and I often laughed at her newest antics, as she invented many more reasons to stay up as long as possible.

"One more story, upstairs," he said, lifting Cary from his lap and looking at his watch, "Say goodnight to Mommy and Lindsay." After our nightly round of goodnight kisses and my reminder to Cary, to "say your prayers," I went into the kitchen, still holding our crying baby.

Thinking that a warm bottle with an ounce or two of her formula and half a crushed aspirin might comfort Lindsay, I prepared it. Like most mothers of young children, I'd learned to do things with one hand while holding a baby in the other arm. By the time Cary was in bed and Don came downstairs and into the kitchen, a glass bottle of infant formula was heating in a pan of water on the stove.

The kitchen was warm and welcoming, though the wind still howled outside. The pleasant scent of the turkey breast I'd roasted for supper lingered. Don leaned against a counter and pulled a cigarette from the pack in his shirt pocket. At the quick flash of his cigarette lighter's flame, Lindsay's attention was caught and she briefly stopped fussing. But not for long. Could I ask Don to hold the baby so I could use both hands? I wondered.

Don had long since made me aware that holding an overwrought baby would not be something he'd prefer to do. Especially, he wouldn't hold a baby who might spit up. In the 1950's it was the mother's established job to take over the entire care of children. The father was the head of the house, the business man and breadwinner.

Don rarely changed clothes when he came from the office. He'd shed his jacket, tie and shoes, but he still wore his impeccable white shirt and creased trousers of his business suit. He wouldn't want to chance the baby's soiling his clothing.

Surprising me that night, my husband *did* tamp out his cigarette in the ashtray on the counter. He studied Lindsay with concern. He reached his arms out to us. "I can hold her if you think you should call the doctor," he said, adding, "He'll probably tell you to give her an aspirin in warm milk and if she's not better in the morning, bring her to the office." It was considered to be a doctor's solution for many baby problems. The words were often jokingly quoted among young parents. Don was trying to lighten my worries with his usual off-the-cuff wit and for a few minutes he succeeded.

"Or check your Spock 101," he said, referring to the text book of a course in Baby and Child Care that I'd taken at the university. Don regularly teased me about the class and particularly about Dr. Spock, my dependable and constantly used guide to the care and rearing of children. The book's pages were well-thumbed and wrinkled, whole paragraphs were underlined, the back cover was held together with Scotch tape, Don called it "the Spock bible."

"Will I Be on Television?"

We agreed that aspirin mixed with some of the baby formula might solve Lindsay's problem. We decided to wait to call the doctor until we'd tried it.

In the early 1950's, doctors still made house calls and we were in the habit of never calling our doctor except for a true emergency, especially at night when they would have to leave their homes and families.

While I painstakingly crushed an aspirin tablet between two spoons and measured half of it, we talked of times that Cary had been fussy. We talked about the baby problem Colic. Colic was a mystery to me, but I knew that it could come on for no reason and cure itself for no reason. Nevertheless, our baby's fretfulness didn't seem to fit the description of colic. It seemed different somehow. Still, we didn't think her problem was an emergency.

Lindsay opened her mouth for the teaspoon of aspirin and formula, but grimacing and pursing her lips at the taste she spit it out. She twisted her head away from a second spoonful. Much later, more formula from her bottle without the added drug seemed to calm her. For a short time she settled down but when I tried to put her to bed she was agitated again.

Eventually Don went to bed, reminding me that he had an early morning meeting. "I wish I knew the answer," he said. "It's too late now to call the doctor, but if she's no better in the morning, you probably should take her to his office." On his way to our bedroom he turned out most of the lights. The house darkened.

With my baby in my arms I settled on the living room couch, hoping to lull her to sleep. The tender warmth of cuddling my baby in a velvety blanket soothed my concerns somewhat, and Lindsay seemed more relaxed as she listened to my whispered reassurances. She'd stop fretting for a minute or two and her eyelids would droop. Gradually, the pauses between her spasms became longer. She tried to sleep. Sitting in the semi-darkness gently rocking her, I almost stopped worrying. Babies can be fussy for no reason. Nothing could be seriously wrong, I convinced myself. After all, she was our Easter baby.

The fact that Lindsay was born on Easter Sunday, two weeks before she was due, always seemed extraordinary. Our obstetrician had received no advance notice. He was in church and couldn't be reached. A resident doctor delivered our baby with forceps as soon as nurses rushed me into the delivery room. I remembered the day she was born as clearly as if it had happened only the day before.

"Here's your Easter bunny," the resident doctor said, holding her for me to see. "You have a little girl."

When the nurse handed her to me, tucked in a blanket with only her head above its folds, my baby felt like a precious unplanned gift. Her birth, that day, would make every Easter Sunday very special for us. I mused about her doing something important when she grew up. That night, I never could have predicted that anything crucial could be wrong with our Easter child.

Long after Don went to bed, Lindsay fell asleep in my arms. She couldn't keep her tiny eyes open any longer. She was exhausted. Slowly, careful not to awaken her, I carried her into the nursery and laid her on her tummy in her crib. In 1953 pediatricians instructed mothers to be certain that babies slept on their stomachs with their faces turned to the side. It was their strong belief that the position prevented phlegm in the throat from choking. That was Lindsay's position. She was sleeping, seemingly comfortable. I hoped she would sleep through the rest of the night.

The nursery was warm again, and pleasant with the still sweet fragrance of baby powder and lotion. White eyelet curtains caught a glint of light from the moon and the hazy lights made the painted toy animals on the walls seem to dance. The wind had died down and a few stars were visible in the night sky.

After Lindsay was settled, and without turning on a light, I navigated the short hallway to Don's and my bedroom. I felt my way through the shadows and slipped into bed, trying not to rouse my sleeping husband. His profile reflected the moon's light coming through our window and the warmth of his body comforted me. I fell asleep.

About six o'clock in the morning I got up. Still half-asleep I checked on Lindsay. Usually she was wide awake, agitating for her morning bottle. That morning she slept. Her breathing was heavier than usual, but she appeared to be comfortable.

When she did awaken, about a half-hour later, my speculation about last night's problem seemed like the right one. Her nose was stuffy. She had a cold, but her temperature was normal and she drank her entire bottle of formula. I didn't think it was necessary to call the doctor. With quiet, extra rest and continuing doses of crushed aspirin mixed with her food, I believed that our baby would get over a simple cold in a day or so.

After breakfast, for more than an hour Cary and I played with dolls and worked jigsaw puzzles, sitting cross-legged on the living room carpet. Lindsay watched us, propped up by a pillow on the couch nearby. She was sleepy, dozing from time to time, but not at all fretful. Less concerned, I went back to my morning routine of chores and checked periodically to be sure she was all right.

The photograph of our wedding caught my glance and made me smile, as it always did. Don and I were a typical post WWII couple. Don, a returned navigator in the Air Force, was discharged in 1945, the year I was a naive freshman at the University of Minnesota. We met on the staff of the Journalism School's daily newspaper. He looked especially handsome in his uniform. He was a four years older than I was, smoking a pipe, self-confident, and seeming in full command of his surroundings.

Don became Sports Editor of the paper. I was Society Editor. We had great fun trying to outdo each other in column space. He was a fierce competitor, winning regularly with the most news. Until the day I covered a two-page feature story. "Enjoy it," he told me. "It may never happen again." It didn't.

Don graduated a year ahead of me. He was hired for the advertising job he'd coveted throughout college. Following my graduation and our traditional wedding celebration, we began life together with an equally traditional honeymoon. Don later described those first two weeks together, "Two of us went on our honeymoon and three came back," he said. Nine months later, in the midst of a January blizzard, Cary was born.

Lindsay was born when Cary was a few months past three. Adding one more baby in the next few years, a boy for Don I hoped, we would be the all-American family, as painted by the artist Norman Rockwell and portrayed on television. All the required pieces appeared to be in place. My husband had the job he'd wanted. Cary and Lindsay were healthy and happy. We were a comfortable and contented family.

I was touched by a wave of sentimentality as I glanced at our wedding photograph. That morning I believed that nothing could destroy the perfect life I projected for us to fill the years ahead.

After lunch, I put both girls to bed for their afternoon naps. Cary was in her upstairs room and Lindsay was in her crib. I debated about calling the doctor just to be safe. Still, Lindsay seemed to be much better. Her temperature was normal. Sleep, I believed, was the right medicine to help her get over her cold. I, too, lay down on the bed in our bedroom and closed my eyes for a few minutes. After little sleep the night before those minutes were welcome. I relaxed as the night's worries about our baby's fretfulness faded.

In less than a half-hour, the afternoon sun through the open window awakened me from my catnap. I could feel its pleasant

"Will I Be on Television?"

warmth on my bare legs on the coverlet atop our bed. I was in no hurry to get up since I thought my four-month-old baby was sleeping peacefully in her nursery a few steps down the hall. I knew that her extra sleep would help whatever recovery might be necessary. The house was quiet. Cary still napped. Don wouldn't be home from work for at least two hours.

When I heard no sounds from either child, I lay on the bed a few minutes longer, still weary from my night of walking the floor with Lindsay. It was well after midnight when she'd finally given in to sleep. Soon, I looked at my watch and realized it was time to begin preparations for dinner. I sat on the edge of the bed and slipped into my loafers. I still heard no sound from either child.

Nothing, ever again, will be as sharp and clear in my memory as what happened from that moment on. I stopped and listened for a minute or two at the half-opened door of Lindsay's nursery. I heard none of the usual stirring sounds indicating she was awake and felt reassured. I was glad that Lindsay was still sleeping and didn't want to disturb her. I continued on toward the kitchen.

To this day, I don't know what made me turn back. I had no warning of danger, only the sense that my baby might be napping overly long. I went into the nursery and to her crib. Lindsay lay motionless, face up. She was shockingly bright blue from head to toe. She wasn't breathing.

The room was a blur. I shivered in shock. Seconds mattered. I had to make Lindsay breathe. Sheer instinct took over. All I could think of was the way doctors started newborns breathing.

I ripped off Lindsay's diaper and grabbed her by the feet. I turned her upside down and smacked her bottom, hard. She cried. Her cry was sharp. She gasped and fought for breath. I struggled against panic until she began to breathe again.

I didn't know I was crying until the blanket that snuggled my baby felt wet in my grip. I couldn't stop shaking. Had I not been able to revive her, Lindsay would have died.

Most infants do not survive Sudden Infant Death Syndrome. It occurs without warning. If Lindsay's close call had happened while I slept, I might not have found her in time to save her.

My baby was still alive. My mind was racing. I tried to think minute by minute. Should I call the doctor? Who would take care of Cary if I left the house? Could I call Don at the office? I brushed questions aside. Terrified that Lindsay might stop breathing again, I wrapped her in her blanket, put her in her basket and grabbed Cary by the hand. We rushed to the car and sped to the nearest hospital.

We Didn't Know
What We Didn't Know

With Lindsay's canvas travel-basket on one arm and Cary hanging onto my other hand, I ran to the garage. How I managed to pull open the heavy garage door, put the girls in the car, back out and drive from our alley to the street, remains a blurred memory.

I raced to Northwestern hospital ignoring the speed limit. Lindsay was still breathing. I remember thinking, *Thank goodness it's a carpool day for Don and our car is available.*

Speeding down quiet suburban streets, I wished a police car would stop me. If one did, I'd have an escort to the hospital. Mostly, Lindsay dozed, breathing normally again. She was tucked in her basket on the front seat beside me where I could watch her. On the backseat, Cary steadied herself as we careened around corners. In those days there were no seatbelts or child's car seats for protection.

I tried to calm myself so I wouldn't frighten Cary, but a terrifying urgency gripped me. When a lumbering yellow school bus loomed directly in front of our car, I didn't know what to do. I couldn't pass it. I was afraid to take the time to stop.

The bus's red lights flashed. Two stop signs swung out from its side. Air-brakes sighed heavily. I could smell the exhaust. The huge vehicle completely blocked my way and I had no choice but to stop. Frantic, with my right arm thrust out to protect Lindsay's basket from falling forward, I slammed on the brakes.

Chattering school children with book bags on their shoulders poured from the open bus doors. In our car Lindsay's cherub face turned up toward me. My heart clutched with worry. I reached over to touch her cheek and fiddle with her blanket to make sure she was covered. Her tiny face didn't seem overly warm. She responded to my touch. I was grateful. Lindsay was alive. *Someday she will be one of those happy youngsters,* I thought. I tapped my foot on the floor mat impatiently, willing the bus to move. *Finally!* The bus doors closed behind the smallest little girl. She'd come down the steps with a helping hand from the driver. The bus moved sluggishly away from the curb and turned down a side street. From then on, nothing slowed our race to the hospital's emergency room.

When we ran through the opened door the woman behind the Information Desk must have seen the look on my face. Her response was quick and concerned as she punched a bell. "My baby stopped breathing," I shouted. A nurse appeared from seemingly nowhere.

"She's all right now," I told her nervously. "I started her breathing but she could stop again."

"We'll get her right into a croupette," the nurse said, reaching to take the infant carrier from my hand. I didn't know what a croupette was, but I didn't take time to ask. Lindsay lifted her head slightly and looked at me as the nurse turned toward nearby double doors and disappeared. A hospital volunteer brought Cary a drink and a child's book while I filled out admission forms. Another volunteer, approaching with a smile, asked Cary. "Would you like to come with me when your mother goes to the nursery to visit your sister?" To me she said, "They'll call you as soon as your baby is settled. It shouldn't be long before you can go upstairs." It seemed to take forever before the call came, but it may not have been more than ten minutes. To my mind the minutes seemed like hours.

"Will I Be on Television?"

After a quick hug and wave to Cary, I hurried to a nearby elevator that took me to the fourth floor pediatric service. Its doors opened onto a wide corridor lined with children's drawings tacked on the walls. Down the hall, I could see the nursery as I hurried past a wall filled with children's drawings. One of them, a stick figure family, colored green, blue and orange, caught my eye as I rushed past. Some of the hospital room doors were closed. Others were partly open. In one, a child sat up in bed surrounded by balloons. In the hallway nurses hovered over charts attached to carts filled with medications.

The nursery's waist-high window was at the farthest end of the long corridor. Its window overlooked a large brightly lit room and rows of white plastic bassinettes. Many held tiny sleeping babies. Others looked ready for use. The bassinets were lined and draped with soft white blankets.

I hoped I'd see Lindsay in the room, but I couldn't identify her among the other babies. I did see a bassinette tented with a clear plastic hood, the inside misted with humidity. *This must be the croupette the nurse talked about*, I thought. But I couldn't tell if it was Lindsay under the misted hood. A nurse was busying herself checking the bassinette and wiping the damp outside of the hood. Every few minutes she'd look up at the window. She must have realized I was Lindsay's mother, for when she saw me she pointed at the basket. I could see the shadow of my baby inside on her back with her tiny hand near her cheek. She looked small and vulnerable. It had to be Lindsay. I longed to hold her. I longed to be sure that no lasting harm had come from her brush with death.

Shortly a door opened behind me and a tall uniformed nurse came toward me. "We've called your pediatrician," she said. "We have Dr. Clarke's instructions to keep Lindsay in the croupette through the night.

"How is my baby?" I asked her.

"She's breathing well," she said. "The croupette supplies oxygen and is helping her breathe normally." She patted my arm to comfort me. I understood that the nurses and Dr. Clarke believed that this mechanical bassinette was the solution for Lindsay's protection from further danger. "Is it a cold?" I asked.

"It's hard to tell," she said. We talked for a few minutes more until the nurse said, "I suggest that you go home and get some rest. Your baby's in good hands now." As terrifying as my baby's condition had been, I then believed it was no more than a temporary illness. Lindsay had seemed like herself when she started breathing once more before we drove to the hospital and when she lifted her head in the lobby.

I collected Cary from the children's room where she was coloring with the companionship of the volunteer and we headed for home. As I drove, I felt relieved and at last able to sort out my thoughts. For the first time since Lindsay's crisis, I wondered if the open heart valve, discovered at birth, could have caused her problem. We'd been told that one heart valve hadn't closed as completely as it should.

But her pediatrician told us, "The condition is not uncommon. It won't cause your baby a problem. It can be corrected with surgery that should be done before she is twelve years old."

"Shouldn't the surgery be immediate?" I'd asked him.

"It's necessary to wait until Lindsay's body is more fully formed. But you mustn't wait any longer than when she is twelve. If you do, let me give you an example of what can happen. It will be like a clock that stops. When you don't wind a clock, it slowly runs down. That's what would happen to Lindsay's heart if she doesn't have surgery to close the valve by the time she's twelve."

Shortly after that conversation we'd changed pediatricians and switched to Dr. Clarke, whose office was nearer our home. I told Dr. Clarke about Lindsay's open heart valve during our first visit. It was never brought it up again. Before Lindsay's emergency I hadn't been concerned about it. Though I did want

Lindsay to have the necessary surgery as soon as her doctor told us the time was right.

When Cary and I arrived home I took her up to her bedroom and tucked her under the covers to rest before dinner. She'd missed most of her afternoon nap. Don came home soon afterward. Without Cary present, we could talk more freely. I told him about Lindsay's emergency. Shocked, but reassuring, he said, "The baby will be fine. She's in good hands. You mustn't worry. You saved her life."

Dr. Clarke called later, explaining Lindsay's need to be in the hospital for a longer time to be certain she'd recovered completely. That call was as comforting to me as the nurse in the hospital had been. In the 50's we trusted that doctors would share information important to their patients. I believed that if a serious problem was of concern, Dr. Clarke certainly would have told me. I had no reason to think that anything might be permanently wrong with my baby.

Unexpectedly, about midnight the Fall weather turned ugly. Both Don and I awakened after midnight to the force of a gale howling around the corners of the house. Unable to go back to sleep, we lay in bed and talked about what had happened that day. "What made you go into Lindsay's room when you thought she was sleeping?" Don asked.

"I don't know. It was the strangest feeling I had that something wasn't right. I've wondered about it myself."

"We're so lucky you found her in time." His confidence relaxed me enough so that tired as I was, I fell asleep soundly and didn't awaken until seven o'clock the next morning.

Early that morning, while Don and Cary still slept, I quietly dressed. Because it was a Saturday, Don planned to stay home with Cary so I could spend time at the hospital with Lindsay. I donned a raincoat, grabbed an umbrella and opened the back door to a wind that almost took the door out of my grasp. The downpour I stepped into was wicked; rain sheeted horizontally.

I drove to the hospital with headlights on and windshield wipers going full bore. The downpour hadn't let up when I reached the hospital's entrance. If anything, it was heavier. I sloshed through deep puddles as I ran to the protective canopy that shielded the doors. A man and woman stood just inside, shaking water from umbrellas. Water pooled at their feet. They were medical staff members going on duty.

Perhaps, because it was early on a weekend, few staff members had arrived...I saw only two more, both nurses. One was behind the desk on the fourth floor and the other was pushing a cart of meds down a hall of patients' rooms. The nurse at the desk looked up from her papers.

"I brought my baby in yesterday. She's in the nursery. How is she? May I see her?" I said, running my questions together in my eagerness to see Lindsay.

When I told her Lindsay's name, she asked me, "Have you talked to your doctor this morning?"

"I expect him to be here for rounds later today," I told her, as she reached for a rack of files on her desk and pulled out a folder. After studying it, she said, "Lindsay's been in a croupette all night. She may be out of it this morning. I'll check." The nurse came back in a few minutes and told me, "They think Lindsay will be all right if she's out of the croupette for a short while, but it will take a little longer to get her ready for you." While I waited, I walked up and down the hallway without seeing another nurse or staff member. Through the nursery window I could see two nurses changing diapers and feeding babies.

After what seemed like a long time, one of the nurses came out with Lindsay in her arms. Wrapped in a white hospital blanket, Lindsay seemed to be sleeping peacefully. Still holding my baby, the nurse led me away from the medical station down a long empty corridor. We walked past a number of vacant rooms. At the far end of the hall we entered a dingy storeroom with ugly gray painted walls. It was empty and looking unused. The room was lighted with a single bare ceiling bulb. A lone metal chair stood in the middle of the room. Bent metal shelves were propped against one wall, most were empty. Dirt clogged the cracks in the linoleum floor. The heavy rain pelted against an unwashed floor to ceiling window.

Pointing to the chair, the nurse said, "You can sit there." *Why am I in this bare storage room?* I wondered. *Why weren't we in one of the more comfortable vacant places? I felt hidden away.*

I started to ask the nurse, but before I could get the question out she spoke abruptly, "If you need me, I'll be down the hall." She handed Lindsay to me and turned to leave the room. I reached out, eager to hold and cuddle my daughter. When I looked up, the nurse was gone.

The minute I took Lindsay from the nurse, I realized that something was terribly wrong. She was heavy, like a lead weight in my arms. Her body was rigid. Her face was expressionless. Her eyes weren't focusing on me. I moved her blanket and her position to see if she'd react. She didn't. I talked to her. She heard nothing. *This cannot be my baby,* I was sure of it. She was so unlike the Lindsay I knew that I checked her plastic wristband and read the tag. In horror, I saw that the wristband held her name. This baby *was* my daughter.

Bewildered and holding Lindsay in my arms, I quickly walked out the door, seeking the nurse to explain what was wrong. The corridor was empty. Only one other person was visible, at the far end of the hall. She disappeared into a room.

I went back to sit on the chair and wait for someone to come. I gently tried to work with my baby, changing her position, lifting her. She didn't respond to my moving her. She didn't respond to my voice. Her eyes didn't follow me. Fear terrified me. The ache and emptiness in my body was indescribable. I couldn't make myself believe that this was the same baby I'd left in the hospital's care.

When I'd handed her to the nurse the day before, she seemed to have almost recovered. Through the night, nurses certainly must have checked her constantly.

I remembered that Lindsay had lifted her head when I handed her basket to the staff member in the lobby. Confident that she'd recovered from her crisis, I believed it was safe to leave her in trusted medical hands. Now she lay in my lap not moving. She didn't responding to my caresses or my voice. Her lack of normal reaction was torturing. What was wrong with her? *What happened to my baby overnight?* All the relief I'd felt turned to horrifying dread.

On this early Saturday morning no one was available to explain the change in my baby. Dr. Clarke would not be at the hospital until afternoon. Carrying Lindsay, I got up from my chair once more to look for someone. The hallway was empty as far as I could see. No one was at the nurses' station. *Why didn't anyone come to check on us?* Not knowing what else to do, I sat down again and cradled my baby, still trying to create some response. The slashing storm outside banged against the window in that dingy dark room. Terrified and alone in the strange ugly place I wept.

With Lindsay not moving in my arms and a sodden handkerchief in my hand I strained to regain my earlier feeling of optimism. Certainly, a baby born on Easter Sunday would recover completely. I stubbornly hung onto that hope.

A Shattering Diagnosis

*D*istraught and heartbroken, I clung to whatever optimism I was able to muster. My plan was to call Dr. Clarke for an explanation as soon as I could reach a phone. I wasn't ready to accept what I'd just seen as permanent, for when Lindsay started breathing again and when I brought her to the hospital, she was the baby I knew. She wasn't at all stiff and unresponsive. There were too many questions and no immediate answers. I stopped looking for a nurse or doctor in the hall and carried my baby back to the nursery to return her to the croupette. I left the hospital.

My mind was in a fog. On the way to the car, I stumbled over a curb I didn't see and almost fell. During the drive home I berated myself for not discovering Lindsay's problem before she stopped breathing. *Why didn't I wake sooner from my nap? Why didn't I check Lindsay more often? Why didn't I call Dr. Clarke the night before?* My guilty feelings were unbearable. Long after that day, I learned that feelings of guilt are not uncommon among parents of handicapped children.

It was early afternoon when I arrived at home. The storm had abated and Don was pushing Cary on her swing in the backyard. I had too much on my mind to say more than a quick "hi" as I passed them on the way to the back door and went into the house and right to the phone.

Dr. Clarke wasn't in his office, but when he called back, he remained non-committal, just as the night before. "I'll be at the

Jan Amis Jessup

hospital later today," he said. He brushed aside my first words when I tried to ask about the symptoms I'd seen.

"Please call me after you see her," I begged. Dr. Clarke did call later but all he said was, "Lindsay's about the same." Again, I tried to probe, but my question was parried. *Why won't medical professionals talk to patients as if they are educated adults?* I wondered, frustrated.

Still not understanding, I interpreted Dr. Clarke's silence as reassuring, simply because I wanted so much to do so. I put my questions aside until later. There seemed to be no reason to persist seeking answers that I wasn't going to get.

Thanks to Lindsay's improvement each following day, I assured myself that her chilling symptoms were temporary. When I held her in my arms, she was almost the baby I knew. She wasn't as she had been that morning in the hospital, not heavy and stiff, not so utterly unresponsive. *Certainly any remaining problems also would disappear.* I continued to believe. I denied my foreboding.

In four days my daughter was more like herself. She moved in my arms and reacted to me. We brought her home from the hospital and I hoped all danger was past. If there were changes in her behavior, they were subtle. I sometimes wondered if Lindsay was holding her head up as firmly as she had before her trauma, or if her eyes were as bright and inquisitive. But my memory of her earlier muscle strength and and the brightness of her eyes was not clear, so I couldn't be certain. Because our pediatrician didn't seem alarmed, I put my own concerns aside. Her crisis passsed and our lives proceeded normally. It was as if the emergency had never happened. My care of our two tots and my pleasure in homemaking caused the days to move swiftly.

It was a peaceful time in America. WWII was in the past, the future was bright. Veterans pursued career opportunities, mothers stayed home and cared for the children. Families gathered for

"Will I Be on Television?"

potluck suppers and barbecues. Kids played all sorts of games out-of-doors until dark, answering to whistles when it was time to come home. It was a happy period for our family. It would be a time to be recalled years later with twinges of nostalgia.

My concerns about Lindsay remained dormant until she was eight months old. Then I became more worried than I had been earlier. Those worries had been growing slowly. Lindsay wasn't as advanced as Cary at the same age, or as active. From birth, she'd been a placid baby, not inquisitive or self-motivating, but we didn't question her differences. More aware of them as the months moved on, I spent extra time playing with her to encourage her motor progress. She loved the attention and eagerly responded to everything we tried together.

I turned to Dr. Spock's book, searching for information about the normal baby development I'd taken for granted with Cary. But I found nothing that applied to Lindsay. The Spock theory was over-simplified, "don't worry if your baby diverges from the norm. Instead, if you let your child set its own pace a comfortable pattern will result." The Spock method produced happier babies and less stressed parents, but his book didn't answer my questions.

The next logical source of help was our pediatrician. But during monthly appointments, Dr. Clarke was still close-mouthed. He would examine Lindsay carefully, rarely saying more about her. I respected Dr. Clarke and since his answers to my concerns were, "I see no change," or, "she's the same as usual," I didn't press further. After checking my baby and giving her shots, he'd say, "I'll see her in a month," and leave the examining room hastily for the next patient.

In my heart, I didn't want to hear that Lindsay's slower growth was a problem, for I believed that if anything was wrong, it was my fault. I tried to put my doubts in the back of my mind and enjoy Lindsay as the loving cooperative baby she was.

Still, by the time she was nine months old other examples of her differences plagued me. Lindsay couldn't sit up by herself. I compared her progress to the children of my friends. Lindsay's was slower, though no one else appeared to notice or talk about it. I didn't talk about her either, believing that if I put my fears into words I might learn they were true.

As sometimes happens in Minneapolis in late February one or two warm days lure residents into thinking that spring may not be far behind. One of those false spring days presented a fine opportunity. For the first time in months I could hang freshly washed laundry out to dry.

Lindsay was content in her small canvas baby seat, just inside our screened porch where I could watch her from where I worked outside. She could see me as I strung wet sheets on clotheslines in the backyard. Often, I stopped what I was doing and came close to the outside of the screen. If a screen hadn't been between us I could have touched her. I'd chatter to her for a few minutes to remind her I was nearby.

At first, I didn't notice anything unusual about her. I was enjoying the out-of-doors, the warming weather and seeing a few jonquils poke their heads above the melting snow. But the next time I went to her I was shocked by what I found. Lindsay's face was entirely bland, expressionless and emotionless. Her eyes wouldn't follow my movements though I did my best to get her attention. She was staring at some far distant place. She didn't react to my voice. She was awake, but unmoving, appearing to be in a trance.

Frightened, I dropped my laundry basket on the ground, raced inside to my baby and lifted her into my arms. When I picked her up she responded just as she usually did. She was the baby I knew. Relieved and able to relax, I stayed with Lindsay for the rest of the day. Thank goodness, her reactions were normal. Still, we could no longer ignore that Lindsay was in trouble. Confident that proper diagnosis and medical care could correct

"Will I Be on Television?"

whatever the problem might be, I knew we had to be serious about finding out the diagnosis.

Was Dr. Clarke not telling me something we should know? How could I pin him down, or was it time for another medical opinion?

For nearly a month we were flying blind, not knowing where or how to find pertinent information or locate the right professional to consult. The only doctor we had was our pediatrician. We didn't have a family doctor because we hadn't needed one. No other source I searched offered any specifics.

It was during a conversation with Don's parents that we heard about Tom, the son of close friends. A recent medical school graduate, he had set up a general practice across town. When I phoned for an appointment, Tom answered the phone himself. He asked, "Is this an emergency?" Without knowing who I was, his sincere tone of caring came through.

"No. It's not an emergency," I identified myself. "I'd like to bring our baby in for an examination."

"I've been hearing about your newest little girl from my folks," he said. "I'm looking forward to seeing you and your daughter."

Lindsay was beginning to wear little girl dresses. The day we kept our appointment, she looked pretty and sweet in her crisp blue and white outfit. She seemed like a special treasure. Tom greeted us cordially and talked pleasantly while I undressed my daughter on the examining table.

In the warm room, Lindsay sat in her diaper and panties while I propped her back with my hand. Tom listened to her heart, talked to her and treated her gently throughout his examination. His friendly manner inspired confidence until he became unusually silent, appearing professional and serious. He looked at me several times as if he wanted to say something, then he looked away, avoiding my eyes.

"Is there a problem?" I asked him. He didn't answer, remaining silent as he handled Lindsay, lifting her tiny fingers and arms, testing her strength. He moved his own finger back and forth in front of her eyes. Again, he turned his face from me. Obviously, something was wrong that he didn't want to talk about.

"Please tell me the problem," I said. Again, he evaded my question. I urged him. "I'd rather know. Please tell me. If we don't know, we won't know how solve it. I can handle it."

At the time I believed I meant what I said, never considering the bombshell he'd drop. I knew that Tom still didn't want to tell me, even when he presented his shattering diagnosis. His ghastly words clearly said, "Your baby will never be normal." My whole body went numb. I must have stood still, in shock. I can't remember how long.

Dazed with disbelief, all I could think of was to run away from his office and his chilling words. Dressing my baby as fast as I could, I thanked him and paid the bill like a mechanical robot going through the necessary motions. Anguished, with Lindsay in my arms and not knowing what to do next, I hugged her tighter as I ran from Tom's building. My tears stained her tiny blue dress. I was stunned and shaking.

The horror of the words he used echoed in my mind. *What Tom said can't be true*, I rationalized. *Lindsay was our miracle child born on Easter Sunday.* But if Tom was right, every dream for my child had just been crushed. My heart held a chilling fear. I desperately needed someone to tell me that Tom was wrong.

Seeking comfort, I drove to my mother-in-law's house. She knew Lindsay well. She had never mentioned a problem. She lived nearby and was usually found working in her garden. I paid scant attention to the cars parked in front of her house and when she answered the ring of her doorbell, I gasped, "Something's terribly wrong with Lindsay!" She looked at me and my baby, obviously disturbed. "My bridge club's here," she said. She took us in and sat with us briefly in a room apart from her guests. She listened as I recounted the doctor's diagnosis. Then, recommending that I go home and call my husband, she abruptly sent us on

"Will I Be on Television?"

our way. I knew she must care. I knew, too, that she didn't want the ladies of her bridge club to hear me.

After that, I drove around, going nowhere in particular until it seemed aimless. When we finally went home I couldn't repeat what I'd heard from Tom and I didn't call Don. Later, somewhat calmer, I collected Cary from nursery school where she'd been while I kept the doctor's appointment.

In a haunting mental vacuum, I took care of the girls and prepared dinner. *Tom couldn't be right,* I assured myself. By the time Don came home I'd almost convinced myself that another opinion would correct Tom's impossible diagnosis. Nevertheless, when my husband walked in the door I burst into tears.

"What's wrong?" he asked, startled.

"Something's wrong with Lindsay." I said as I told him about our appointment. Don listened, remaining non-committal. I wasn't surprised, my husband rarely shared his emotions. Rather, when confronted with a problem a tiny vein in his forehead would throb. It began to throb as I recounted the details of the day. Don often avoided serious conversation. His preference was to turn a difficulty into laughter. So many times it soothed a troubling situation. That evening, with no possibility of anyone being soothed, he didn't try.

We hardly talked, except Don asked, "Has Dr. Clarke told you anything like this?"

"No," I said. Neither Don nor I could think about what to do next.

"There Are Institutions"

I was so convinced that Tom was wrong, I set out to prove it. I didn't know that events and decisions during her early years would frame the rest of my daughter's life.

The obvious first person to talk to about Tom's diagnosis was Dr. Clarke. I put it off because of his earlier avoidance. Instead, I spent hours encouraging Lindsay to sit up. I kept her nearby during my daily chores and involved her with a steady patter. We played baby games. Tucked in her light canvas Teeter-babe, she was easy to move to wherever I was. By her next monthly pediatrician's appointment, she proudly demonstrated her accomplishments for Dr. Clarke, who encouraged me and applauded her progress.

Still wanting to believe that Tom misread Lindsay's problem, I confronted Dr. Clarke directly, and asked him, "What future do you predict for Lindsay?" This time he didn't back off and went into more detail. Though he didn't entirely agree with Tom's drastic observation his words hit me like a bomb, "There are institutions for children like this." It was the first time I heard those horrible words. Sadly, it wouldn't be the last time.

Dr. Clarke's comment was a terrible blow. My impression of institutions was based on two ugly and depressing gray stone buildings I'd driven past from time to time in my home town. One a hospital for tuberculosis patients, the other an orphanage.

For some reason I was more able to process Dr. Clarke's bad news than I had processed Tom's. Still, I pressed on to seek more opinions. What did other doctors observe? What could we do to improve Lindsay's situation? My next visit was to the University of Minnesota's highly regarded medical school where my baby was examined and tested. Though no doctor delved into the cause of Lindsay's slower development, they agreed with Dr. Clarke's recommendation. They confirmed some of Tom's predictions. It wasn't until fifty years later that I was told by a doctor that Lindsay's first frightening symptoms—her heavy weight, stiffness and lack of responsiveness the day after her crisis—were caused by oxygen deprivation.

The University staff tried to be helpful, describing why Lindsay's problems could be ongoing. Again, those staff doctors offered, "There are institutions for children like this." A stigma identified the "retarded," and if those children lived at home the stigma adhered to the entire family. It took years for me to realize that these seemingly cruel medical recommendations were signs of the times. They were not meant to be unkind. In the 50's, few general practitioners studied or dealt with mentally impaired children. Examinations required time and money for specialists. Children were frequently sent away. They might be hidden, not educated, not seen in public, nor talked about. They were treated as non-persons, thought of as a family's shame. Countless years later a famous playwright's son was brought out of an institutional "closet," where he'd spent the years since he was a small child. His mother was the only one who acknowledged him.

While the doctors I consulted considered Lindsay a *case*, I knew her as a vulnerable little girl I loved, who had a big heart and looked no different from other children her age. I knew the baby who eagerly tried with all her ability to achieve whatever I asked of her. The extra time I spent with Lindsay was proving to make a difference, but keeping her home caused other problems.

The time I spent with Lindsay was beginning to detract from the time and attention needed by Don and Cary. Cary staged an unlikely way to let me know. Usually the 'little mother' to

"Will I Be on Television?"

Lindsay, Cary began to be naughty. Ignited by the loss of my attention, one day she balked angrily at taking a nap. "You're going to play with Lindsay," she said. "Why can't I play with her, too?" When I insisted that she needed her nap, she trudged furiously to her room and busied herself cutting paper dolls out of the fabric shades I'd pulled down over her windows. Her message was quite clear.

From that time on Cary was included in my time spent with her sister. Thus began a remarkable bond between the two girls. It has continued throughout the years. Cary deserves infinite credit for her sister's self-confidence, emotional intelligence and personality.

On the other hand, Don slowly withdrew. He absented himself from every appointment for Lindsay, never asking about tests or showing any interest in possibilities that could lead to improving her life.

Though Dr. Clarke devastated me by talking of institutions, he did Lindsay a favor by telling me about Sheltering Arms. Founded in the late 1800's, it became a hospital for polio victims. When it was no longer needed as a hospital, its trained psychologists began to work exclusively with mentally impaired children. The staff could evaluate Lindsay's development and guide me in planning for her future. At that time it appeared that Lindsay might be catching up. She seemed to do most of what our friends' toddlers were doing. Though slower, Lindsay loved other children and tried to play with them. I believed that the psychologists at Sheltering Arms would see the positives I saw in Lindsay's eager attempts.

Our appointment at Sheltering Arms was in the spring of the year Lindsay was three. More than ever, she was a happy-go-lucky delightful little girl, easy and undemanding. Always excited by new adventure, she beamed at being dressed up and riding in the car. As we rounded a curve on the grassy shore of the Mississippi River, I recognized a stately red brick building surrounded by handsome gardens. I'd driven past the campus-like area many times but never before realized the building was Sheltering Arms.

In a sunny vestibule, a tall woman in a crisp white blouse and navy skirt greeted us by name as we came through the door. At first, she spent a few minutes talking to Lindsay. Never shy, Lindsay was happy, welcoming her as a new friend. The psychologist put us both at ease immediately. She introduced herself as Barbara Parsons and led us into an inviting room filled with children's tables and chairs. Low shelves overflowed with youngsters' books and toys. "Let's have Lindsay sit here," she said, pointing to a place on the carpet near the middle of the room. She selected toys from the shelves and scattered them near my daughter. She then spent a few minutes with me.

Shortly, Miss Parsons picked up a clip-board and pencil from the nearest table and appeared to be preparing to sit on the floor with Lindsay. "There's a lovely parlor across the hall where I know you will be comfortable while you wait," she told me.

"You'll find coffee, some cookies and magazines. Please, help yourself. This will take about an hour and a half, maybe a bit longer," she said as she directed me across the hall to a library and closed the examination room door.

For the next ninety minutes I was optimistic, confident that this psychology staff would direct me in a plan for Lindsay's development. My daughter was so responsive that I didn't doubt Miss Parson's working to reverse other doctors' implications. Again, I was wrong. She presented the facts more kindly and explained them more carefully. Nevertheless, they were facts. "But Lindsay is doing so much better now," I defended my daughter.

"Yes, she is doing well and she is a sweet little girl," Miss Parsons smiled. "I hope she will remain just that," she said. "You may not see obvious changes for a while." There was sympathy in her expression. She turned pages on her clip board and said, "Let me show you a chart."

"Will I Be on Television?"

She held up a graph with lines at the left side of the paper, an eighth of an inch apart. Along the bottom of the page were figures, 1,2,3, depicting the years of Lindsay's life. Miss Parsons pointed to those lines. "You see," she said. "At an early age Lindsay's development will be quite similar to that of other small children. That's where she is now. I looked farther to the center of the graph and saw that the lines gradually diverged. One line ascended, the other remained flatter, only slowly ascending.

"I believe I understand what you're telling me," I said.

"Yes," she looked up from the graph. "Other youngsters will progress at a normal pace, while Lindsay will not. As she becomes older the differences between her ability and theirs will become more marked."

"Will she fit in? What will her life be like? Will she ever be happy?" I asked. For a brief minute I felt as I did when I ran from Tom's office. It was all so wrong. Did anyone expect something like this when they had children? Did they give it thought? I saw Miss Parsons watching me and caught myself.

"Can you, or a staff member, work with us to bring Lindsay to the level she can achieve?"

"I'm so sorry," she said, sympathetically. "We aren't equipped to do that. She, too, added the option, "There are institutions." Miss Parson tried to be optimistic. She said to continue to work with Lindsay, encourage her. She was the first professional who hadn't been entirely clinical or cynical. She didn't say that Lindsay could be helped, but she didn't say she couldn't, either.

Although, "There are institutions for children like this," was the only option doctors offered, it was an option I could not accept. True, Lindsay's progress was slow, but she developed a winsome charm as she grew. Like a playful kitten, she scampered through the days, weeks and months of her early life. It took almost two years for me to accept the hard truth of Lindsay's permanent handicap. Though because she was only two when I finally faced what lay ahead for her, it was not too late to make informed decisions to help her. My daughter's successful future, despite her limitations, ultimately made me grateful that I woke up and faced the facts as soon as I did. Had I delayed longer in facing the facts of her development, I would have deprived her of the help she needed at her earliest age.

Lindsay, with her usual sprightliness and happy abandon, cooperated in more tests. As Barbara Parsons had done, psychologists made the sessions fun for her by using dolls, toys and coloring books to measure her abilities.

Most tests confirmed Doctor Tom's earlier general diagnosis. Still, the examiners were impressed by Lindsay's pluck and courage. They began to share my belief that there were alternatives to impersonal institutions. There were a few schools that offered educational opportunities.

When Lindsay was two, I was informed that all mentally handicapped children born in Minnesota were required to become Wards of the State. Determined that the State would not dictate Lindsay's life, I applied for a Conservatorship. This meant that I would become her legal guardian as well as her mother. The application required red tape, an attorney, a court appearance and renewal each year. Despite the time, effort and cost involved, it has proved a boon throughout the succeeding years.

By age four, Lindsay was already trying to catch up to her seven-year-old sister. Cary patiently showed her how to button a button and tie a shoe. She would have Lindsay practice with dolls. She turned lessons into games. The two small girls, pretending to be adults in long skirts, veiled hats, with Cary teetering on grown up high heels, entertained each other playing dress-up and having tea parties. If Cary invited her friends to play she included Lindsay in what her sister was able to do.

Frequently, Lindsay couldn't manage what she attempted. Tying her shoes by herself was hard for her. When she climbed on a stool to brush her teeth, she had to cling to the sink for balance. Still, she never gave up, nor did frustration affect her happy

"Will I Be on Television?"

disposition. Seeing my daughter blossom in her own way, despite formidable odds, I knew my decision to keep her with us was the right one.

As she grew other options became more important. Whenever the opportunity arose, I continued consulting psychologists and medical doctors to learn more ways we could help Lindsay. I searched information to make the most of the gifts she had, despite that from some in our family and doctors closest to us, no word of encouragement was offered. Stigma depicting the "retarded" was rife in attaching itself to individuals and touching families. A few members of Don's family feared it. Most troubling was that Don, himself, pulled away from us more and more. He began to find other things to do nights and weekends. Though he'd always enjoyed parties and drank beer at home, his drinking increased. When Lindsay was around, he treated her as if she wasn't there.

I was naive and too emotionally involved with Lindsay's well-being to realize that the stigma could apply to her. I found Don's behavior difficult to understand. *Why wouldn't her father want to help her as I did?* I chalked up the changes to his increasingly successful job in advertising and the job's additional demands. It didn't occur to me that Don's difficulty accepting that we had a handicapped child was because of his self-image. He was embarrassed by Lindsay.

When a kind neighbor, Betty, came into our lives, her complete acceptance of Lindsay made it more difficult for me to understand the reason for Don's changing behavior. I met Betty at a meeting of a local Women's Club. She stood out from the group for her beauty and Southern warmth. We built our second home only a few blocks from hers and our families became close friends. Though the demands of their family-owned company required activity-filled days, Betty went out of her way to fit Lindsay into her schedule. Among other talents Betty was an excellent artist. She used her artistic talent to intrigue my little girl.

At the time, Lindsay struggled with a tremor in her tiny hands, one eye that didn't focus and an obvious lack of coordination. Many others didn't know how to react to my child. Not wanting to hurt Lindsay's or my feelings by saying or doing the wrong thing, they simply pretended she wasn't there. Betty was different. She accepted Lindsay as the delightful, fun-loving little girl she was and catered to her special needs by treating Lindsay just as she treated any other toddler, while making subtle allowances for her learning difficulties.

It was obvious the two shared secrets. I learned about them one day when Betty invited the two of us to join her for lunch. My daughter dropped my hand as soon as she saw Betty. She held her arms out for the hug she knew was forthcoming. Lindsay was determined to have more than one hug and move along to the next anticipated activity. She held onto Betty's hem until she was lifted into her arms and carried toward Betty's artist's studio.

The studio's sliding glass wall overlooked a garden in full bloom and beyond it a quiet lake. Watercolors, oil paintings and large swatches of unusual fabrics were tacked and draped haphazardly on the other walls. Soft music filled the room.

As soon as Betty put Lindsay down, my daughter took my hand and pulled me toward an oilcloth apron hanging on a hook. Covered with dried paint, the apron looked several sized too big for Lindsay. Nevertheless, she let me know she wanted to wear it. With a happy grin she had me put it on her. Never mind that it enveloped her from head to toe. Proud as a peacock, she marched to a low easel and pointed to a large sheet of white paper covered with blue, red, yellow and green lines and squiggles.

"Lindsay, did you paint that beautiful picture?" It was what I was supposed to ask. My daughter couldn't have been more excited. Grinning at me, she clapped her hands and ran to Betty to hug her legs.

"Would you like to show your mother how you paint?" Betty gently took my daughter's hand as she went to the easel and

"Will I Be on Television?"

carefully tore off the painted sheet. Just as carefully she handed Lindsay's painting to me. She attached another blank sheet of paper to the easel. At the same time, Lindsay picked up a brush from the easel's tray. Concentrating like a professional, my daughter painted more bright colored lines and squiggles. Eventually, she was covered with blobs of paint on her face, hands and especially on the apron. But it didn't stop her mile-wide grin when Betty and I exclaimed over her masterpiece. "Lindsay, that's perfectly beautiful!"

"Sweetheart, I had no idea you could paint." I told her. "We'll take your pictures home and put them on your wall." Lindsay clapped her hands. Jumping up and down, she nodded ecstatically.

Betty's hours of devotion to Lindsay taught me that though Lindsay was *different*, she would respond to kindness and understanding just as would any young child. I was led to recall Dr. Seuss' words, *"A person is a person no matter {what}. A person is a person after all."* Watching how Lindsay responded to Betty's kindness and attention, convinced me, all the more, that my daughter deserved every opportunity. Betty showed us that the love of a friend, clothed in patience and creativity, will elicit unexpected strengths in a child, no matter what their capability might be.

"It Didn't Come From Our Side of the Family"

The years after Lindsay's diagnosis were the most emotionally painful I've ever experienced. They lasted from the time she was nine months until she was almost three. I carried the burden of a child "who might never be normal" entirely alone. For a long time I didn't tell anyone about our daughter's diagnosis. I was afraid that if I put it into words it might be true. I was afraid of a stigma. I felt guilty, afraid that I was at fault. Don's mother knew about Lindsay's having a problem. So did Don, but neither one talked about it to me. It was as if we shared a guilty secret.

Dr. Clarke never mentioned the possibility that Lindsay might be impaired. Friends and neighbors our age were having babies of their own and all were healthy. My former schoolmates had normal babies. My baby was *different* and I had no knowledge or experience to draw on. I had no one to talk to. I didn't know where to find direction. I didn't know how to help a baby who wasn't the same as all my friends' babies. I felt as if I'd been dropped into a bottomless void.

During my twenty-four years I could recall meeting only one *mentally retarded* boy, for that's what he was called. He made me uncomfortable. I felt sorry for him and I didn't know how to approach him. Would our daughter be like that boy? Would she be called *retarded?* Would she make other people uncomfortable? At the time Lindsay was an adorable little tot who was eager to please. She enjoyed our working together to encourage her abilities. It was touching to watch her try her best. She giggled when we played.

Don and I were the ones who had to grapple with telling our closest family members what I'd been told about Lindsay. Don backed away from that difficult responsibility, but I felt that I owed Don's mother more of an explanation than what I'd blurted out the day her bridge club members were in her home. When I finally brought up the subject over coffee in her kitchen, her natural reserve kept her emotions in check. But she did have questions. "Do other doctors agree? How can they predict for Lindsay while she's so young? What do you plan to do now?" Don's father, a kind and quiet man, joined our conversation. I had no answers for their questions but I sensed their understanding and support. I believed they would love Lindsay just as they loved Cary.

I left their kitchen feeling better, because I now had someone to talk with about my concerns. Perhaps they would advise me. But that didn't happen. Unless I talked about Lindsay's situation, the subject never came up. To their infinite credit, however, her grandparents always treated Lindsay just as lovingly as they treated our other children, quietly compensating for her special needs. They enjoyed her as she was. Sadly, another family member's reaction was quite the opposite.

Don's maternal grandmother, who lived with his parents, was an important member of our immediate circle. Unbeknownst to me, she had a problem with others' disabilities. An obviously intellectually-impaired boy grew up in the small town she came from. He'd earned a reputation as a known trouble-maker. His family was maligned, avoided and ridiculed. His handicap was blamed for his behavior. Don's grandmother now felt herself placed in the same position as his family. The stigma of a handicapped child reflected on the child's family. The stigma was something someone of her generation couldn't accept. Her subdued rage focused on me.

"Will I Be on Television?"

Long before we told other family members about Lindsay's prognosis, she startled a room filled with relatives by announcing, "It didn't come from our side of the family." I still picture her piercing eyes and features screwed up in fury.

Dumbfounded and in tears over one more hurtful shock about my daughter, all I could manage was, "It didn't come from anybody's side of the family." She didn't hear me. After that, her behavior toward Lindsay and me altered drastically. She avoided us at every opportunity.

Once the sad news of our daughter was known among some, it became necessary to share it with more of our closest relatives. As it was with Don's grandmother, each family member's reactions reflected their own previous experience. Because the branches of my family tree were filled with medical professionals, writers, musicians and other high achievers living in college towns, an intellectually-impaired child was beyond the realm of these relatives' imaginations. All of them lived in other states so the subject of Lindsay never came up.

Fortunately, my parents were an exception. Living four hundred miles away, they were the last to be told about their granddaughter. Though I desperately needed their support, it would have been too harsh to break the news with an impersonal phone call. As expected, when I did tell them, they proved to be the most understanding and sympathetic of all.

They paid extra attention to Lindsay. They applauded each bit of progress she managed. Enchanted by her giggle, my father bounced her on his lap to her great delight. Getting down on the floor with her, he encouraged her to crawl and later to walk. Nevertheless, because of his family background, it took many years for him to acknowledge that anything could be permanently *different* about his adored granddaughter.

Don and his grandmother were the only ones whose behavior changed notably. Don became increasingly distant from the children and me, though he continued to participate in our Sundays and holidays with his parents. Christmas was always a time of great family joy. After months of preparation and the arrival of my mother and father for Christmas week, we celebrated Christmas Eve in Don's folk's home.

During the traditional Swedish Christmas Eve feast the two grandfathers' conspiracies made everyone laugh. They set the table with collapsing forks, provided noisemaker "whoopee" chair cushions and played all sorts of other pranks their imaginations could conjure. The children could hardly sit still. They were tickled by the fun of pulling ribbons from the toy chimney in the center of the dining table and finding a small toy. They knew presents were soon to be found behind the temporary sheet that hung between the dining room and the darkened living room. Fancy wrapped mysteries would be discovered after Santa arrived and the sheet was pulled down. They fairly vibrated with anticipation until the hidden Christmas tree erupted in glorious luminescence, sleigh bells jingled and they knew Santa was at work behind the curtain. Each year he somehow escaped them by minutes. But when Cary was five she was certain he hadn't escaped. When she heard the sleigh bells and the sheet came down she raced to a window shouting, "I saw him! I saw him in his sleigh in the sky!" She created a dear and special family memory we still talk about.

Lindsay participated in the festivities as eagerly as did her siblings. Scant attention was paid to her slower progress. Without a second thought, everyone helped her untie ribbons and open her presents. If it was a toy someone would show her how to play with it. If a little dress, we'd hold it up to her and fuss over how pretty she'd look wearing it. One Chistmas Eve, while everyone else was opening presents, I looked around the living room for her and saw her halfway up the stairs to the bedrooms. She was peeking through the banister at the spirited gaiety below. An image of Christmast spirit in her red and white striped flannel pajamas and tasseled cap, she'd separated herself from the fun. I wondered why.

"Will I Be on Television?"

Was it because she was left behind while the other two children were dashing from one grandparent to another, showing off gifts, clambering up on laps, climbing down again and racing to the tree for their next shiny package? Was she afraid to join the fun because she couldn't keep up with the others? Or did she enjoy her own undisturbed perch where she could observe the scene? Whatever the reason, as I scooped up my little girl several sets of arms opened wide to take her in. Smiling radiantly, she reached out and snuggled into the closest embrace.

With grace, responsibility and understanding, her grandparents treated Lindsay no differently from Cary and our third baby, Bruce. Their gift to all three children was the warmth of their presence, their dreaming up special excursions, and bestowing happiness and contentment on those early childhood years.

As important as this was to Lindsay's development, equally important were her sibling relationships. Earlier when Lindsay was a baby, her three-and-a-half year old sister, Cary, became a little mother. She begged to hold the baby's bottle and tuck her into her crib. As the girls grew, Cary included Lindsay with her own friends. She didn't see her sister as different. Cary and the other little girls played dress-up in clothes from the attic. When Lindsay could walk they dressed her, too. She was delighted to be part of the fun. Dressed in clothes many sizes too large, pinned and tucked to fit, she responded with glee. When the girls had a tea-party, she was the guest. Cary taught her sister to hold a tea cup by gently forming her tiny fingers around the handle until Lindsay could do it by herself.

In pajamas on the living room floor the girls played together early mornings. Cary taught her sister to fit large wooden jigsaw pieces into the proper slots. If Lindsay had trouble, Cary plopped down on elbows and knees to help her. When Cary saw me help Lindsay brush her teeth, tie her shoes, button her buttons or comb her hair, she'd help. These acts of kindness, teaching Lindsay, began close ties that have strengthened and lasted over

Jan Amis Jessup

the years. Living with Lindsay, Cary developed the compassion, patience and creativity that led her to an exceptional career as a teacher. If asked "what is it like to grow up with a mentally-impaired sibling?" Cary will answer, simply and tenderly, "She's my sister." That says it all.

As Lindsay's lack of progress became apparent, we had to learn how to handle gossip on the grapevine about our *different* child. During the early years of ours and our friends' new-parent lives, couples with toddlers and babies in baskets would get together as often as possible in one another's homes or out-of-doors, frequently toting their children with them.

Early on, when I brought the two girls along, Lindsay was no different from the others. Later, her slower development and other signs of her disability became obvious. As her need for help increased, Lindsay became a topic of behind-my-back discussion. Conversation would cease or the subject would abruptly be changed when I was near. Our friends were uncomfortable. I was miserable. Few of our friends knew how to handle a situation they had never encountered before. As uncomfortable as that situation was, it was a tremendous help in determining how to protect Lindsay through future years.

Drawing on my past experience with the boy called *retarded*, I remembered how I didn't know what to do when I met him. I realized how important it was to help others learn to be comfortable with Lindsay and with me. Immediately disturbing about that boy had been his unkempt clothing and lack of personal grooming. I determined that Lindsay would always be clean, well-groomed and well-dressed. I would help her learn the importance of eliminating this barrier to being accepted by others. I remembered not knowing how to approach the boy when we were introduced. What words were suitable? Could he respond? Hoping to prevent others from being in this position with my daughter or

"Will I Be on Television?"

me, I experimented in our groups by paving the way to others' understanding. I began by explaining Lindsay's situation honestly.

"Lindsay is brain-damaged," I'd say, briefly describing her crisis and adding, "But she's our treasure whose life was spared. She will understand what you are saying and will respond to it just as would a child of three (or five, or whatever her intellectual age was at the time). In many situations my introducing the subject of Lindsay's disability was all that was needed. My explanations evoked comments such as "she seems so sweet," or "she doesn't seem so different." People became more comfortable with us. At times they talked to Lindsay and she responded. At times they expressed sympathy. As the years progressed they shared personal or family experiences about handicapped children they knew. In every situation others were more at ease with both of us.

Strangers' reactions were a different challenge. Sometimes their stares made me want to hide my daughter, particularly as her differences became noticeable. At five, her first eye-glasses were sometimes askew. At times they were tangled in her soft blonde hair. Eye-glasses called attention to her face. Often, her fair features were less animated than those of other youngsters. She lacked a child's usual coordination and their quick physical responses and agility.

In those days it was rare to encounter a special needs child in public. In fact, the term 'Special Needs' was un-coined, coming into common usage many years later. In the fifties, most intellectually-impaired children were placed in institutions or secluded at home. They were rarely seen.

My emotions were conflicted. I felt embarrassed, but also over-protective of my innocent daughter. Lindsay was uncomfortable, too. She didn't understand the reason but she clung to my hand in public places. I didn't like myself for my reaction, but I found I was scheduling my errands so I could leave her at home.

Though it took time, my little girl conquered some of those challenges by herself. When we were with a group of friends and their children, Lindsay would be ignored because she couldn't keep up. The youngsters brushed past her and continued playing without her. I was more saddened than Lindsay, until I watched her begin to meet the problem head on. Undaunted, our impetuous child took matters into her own hands. She simply trotted along behind the others, laughing and happy, not at all troubled that she was bringing up the rear. Many times she was helped by one of the other mothers whom she'd won over. Lindsay was far more adept than I was at meeting emotional challenges.

It took me years. I was too self-involved to put aside feelings of guilt, shame and embarrassment because of my daughter. The first person who taught me the subtle beauty of my special child was Betty. Betty made no secret of her love for Lindsay. Her activities with my daughter, their painting, dances to music while she held Lindsay's tiny hands all showed it. Betty taught me, by example, of the wonder of the dear little girl who truly was our gift.

What also led me to work positively with my feelings was an unforgettable evening many years later. During cross-country travels, I visited relatives in a southern city. It was a balmy summer evening, a beautiful time to be out-of-doors. A revival meeting was planned in a park not far from their home. Family members and neighbors decided to attend and invited me to join the large gathering. With curiosity piqued by an event I'd heard described, but never witnessed, I went along.

After a fascinating evening filled with new experience, dusk was moving in as our group prepared to leave the park. Standing in a small cluster at the end of rows of chairs, we were saying goodbyes when my attention was caught by a small girl on the far side of the crowd. Alone and determined, with her hair blowing in the evening breeze, she was making her way through the empty rows and coming directly toward us. She was watching me. As she approached, I could see that she obviously was a child with special needs. It was difficult to tell her age. I didn't know her and had never seen her before that night.

The child walked straight on, until she came very near to me. Our eyes met. When she was close she took hold of my hand. Without a second's thought, I knelt down and hugged her. A smile that pierced my heart lighted her face and brought tears to my eyes. She squeezed my hand tighter. I didn't ask her name. I had no idea why she selected me from the crowd. As I stood up and looked around for her family she darted into the bevy of adults moving toward the exit. I've never forgotten that touching encounter. I've wondered if she somehow sensed that I understood.

From that time on, whenever I'm in a public place and see an impaired person, or a parent with a special needs child or adult, I go to them and smile and speak. That small effort always brings the personal reward of seeing sudden smiles overtake their disquiet. For me, the gift is realizing how much my gesture of friendship is appreciated. Fascinating, as well, is how others follow the lead when one person in a group makes a gesture of friendship to those special children and adults. Others join in. I regret the years it took me to forget my self-concern and to learn the importance of these simple acts of kindness.

"Dogs Can Walk, Too"

Lindsay overcame an enormous hurdle when she learned to walk. I wanted to shout to the world that she was not as handicapped as I'd been led to believe. Could she be developing normally at last?

We had not seen Doctor Tom since his original diagnosis, but because he was the doctor who'd predicted mental retardation, I particularly wanted him to witness her new skill. Surely, after watching her walk he'd agree that her problems were not permanent. I still believed that with proper attention, Lindsay's progress could be almost the same as that of other children.

My first inclination was to hasten the date of her walking debut in order to hear praise of her accomplishment from Tom. My second thought was to delay. A delay would give Lindsay time to gain more strength and better coordination. The latter decision won. Together, we exercised and played games that encouraged Lindsay to be more secure on her little legs. She not only cooperated, she joyfully attempted new heights. In less than a month, I felt assured that her performance would not disappoint Tom or us.

In the early fifties Minneapolis was a homebody small town. Doctors became close friends of the families they treated. Because Tom's parents had been best friends of Don's folks for years, we considered Tom a friend as well. We invited Tom and his wife to our home for dinner. In our home he would be more relaxed than at his busy office. It would be the perfect occasion for Lindsay to perform her recently acquired ability to walk.

Our baby must have sensed that it was a special event when she was dressed in her favorite pink frock and white pinafore with a hair ribbon in her blonde curls. Her face lit up like a sunbeam as she kept pointing to her tiny new white shoes and lace-topped anklets. I was as excited as Lindsay. Held in my arms, she greeted our guests at the door. A short time later she was on the floor taking a few steps alone toward my outstretched hands. I was certain Tom's enthusiasm would match my own. I'd anticipated an evening of mutual celebration. Watching his face, I awaited his expression of surprise and delight.

Instead, he looked me in the eye, almost angry. Abrupt and brutal, he announced, "Dogs can walk, too." Shocked, I must have stared at him. How could anyone, particularly a professional, be so cruel? Or was this Tom's way of telling me again that Lindsay's life was worthless?

Following that dreadful episode I forced myself to face predictions of my daughter's future. Dr. Clarke's, the University medical staffs', and Sheltering Arms' options were "there are institutions for children like this." From Tom, along with the obvious but unspoken reactions of some family members, I translated the message to mean, "Put her away and forget her." But Lindsay was my daughter, my responsibility. I'd grown up in a family that found solutions for problems. I'd been taught that one doesn't run from responsibility. I determined to seek no additional opinions, at least for a while. I continued to encourage Lindsay, watching her and waiting. In turn, she encouraged me, in an unexpected way, by taking the future into her own hands.

Not only did Lindsay's walking improve considerably, she turned it into a happy game for herself. We didn't expect her game to result in great dismay for us.

At one and two years Lindsay was an easy baby, never getting into scrapes as did her older sister. At two, Cary painted a win-

"Will I Be on Television?"

dow with my lipstick, and she delighted in piling pots and pans all over the kitchen floor in order to play drums. Lindsay was quieter, not mischievous. But she made up for those quiet years when she learned to walk at three. She turned into a fearless explorer. Her capricious adventures terrified us. Lindsay didn't understand why we'd worry about her wandering away. Our happy-go-lucky little girl never worried.

Summer afternoons, our two daughters played together, either in our house or in the backyard on the swing set. Lindsay loved motion, dancing, twirling and swinging. She was in her element when one of us pushed her high on the swing or lifted her onto the slide. I took my turn pushing and lifting.

When the time came for my indoor chores, I monitored the girls from a kitchen window. Late one afternoon while they played outdoors, I was inside peeling potatoes for dinner. Cary came into the kitchen for a drink of water. Handing her a glass and talking I looked away from the window, but not for more than a few minutes.

When Cary finished her drink she ran back outside. The screen door slammed. The next thing I heard was Cary's shout, "Mom, Lindsay's gone." I looked out the window and saw that the gate to our fenced yard was wide open. Apparently, Lindsay unlatched it when she was alone. She was nowhere to be seen. In the few minutes we were distracted, Lindsay vanished. Panicked, Cary and I raced through neighborhood backyards and around the block searching for her. I'd go in one direction, Cary in another. We were certain she couldn't have gone far in such a short time, but we saw no sign of her.

"What should we do?" Cary was in tears. Though I, too, was churning inside, I tried to calm her and tell her it wasn't her fault. We had no reason to think that Lindsay had learned to unlatch the gate. We'd never seen her near the gate. We needed a car to search farther away. Ours was in the parking garage at Don's office. By the time I phoned and he came home it would have been too late to trace our small child's trail or to find out if anyone had seen her.

"I'll call the police," I said.

Fortunately, in a quiet suburb such as ours, there was little crime and that day an officer was readily available. A sergeant in a squad car arrived only a few minutes later. With the two of us seated in back, he began an extensive search. He drove ever-widening circles of our immediate area. Reassuring us as we rode, terrified that harm may have come to Lindsay, he said, "She can't have gone far. I'm sure we'll find her. We'll look until we do."

He crept along the nearby streets as each of us scanned the area from our sides of the car. Most of the streets were empty of vehicles or people. Had they been crowded we could easily have missed Lindsay. As tiny as she was, she would have been hidden by any obstruction. But even on the empty streets, we saw no sign of her and there was no one to ask if they'd seen a small child. It seemed an eternity with no success. The officer drove ever farther away from our home.

Not ready to give up, I still had no idea where to turn next when Cary startled us. "There she is. There she is," she exclaimed. I saw Lindsay, too. For both of us the relief was so great it could have been packaged. There was my daughter, her blonde curls bobbing as she merrily tripped up a hill almost six blocks from home. While we marveled at how she got there, she was entirely oblivious of our concern. She was enjoying herself, laughing at nothing in particular and having a glorious time. We understood, viscerally, how heartbreaking it would have been to lose forever our "adorable little tot." No one would ever convince us that this child was worthless.

From then on we were more watchful of our intrepid wanderer. Many times she'd try to slip away from us. She meant no harm. Usually we managed to catch her before she could go far, but we learned to keep her close to us. She was never again outdoors alone. She also had another unexpected protector in our devoted collie.

"Will I Be on Television?"

When we learned that Bruce was on his way our small bungalow seemed to shrink in anticipation of two adults and three children. A move was definitely called for. A trustworthy contractor built us a beautiful home on a small lake surrounded by the back yards of seven other homes. Snowflake became one of my best baby-sitters. Collie dogs are natural herders. In the summer-time, if the children approached too close to the lake from our back yard, Snowy herded from the shore. In winter, when the lake became an ice-skater's paradise, she followed them onto the ice. Sensing Lindsay's need, Snowflake rarely left her side. Their companionship was touching to see. Outside, Lindsay would hang onto Snowflake's ruff and they'd slow-trot together. Inside, she'd curl up on the floor in front of the fireplace with her head on the soft fur of our snoozing collie.

"Why is Snowy barking so?" I asked Cary one evening at dusk when Lindsay was almost five. As Lindsay grew, we believed she was past her 'fearless adventurer' stage. As she became more self-sufficient we became more complacent. There had been no instances of her wandering away for a year. "I don't know why Snowflake's barking," Cary said. "She probably wants to come in." Snowy was outside the half-opened door to our lower floor recreation room, agitated and barking her head off.

"Why don't you let her in," I suggested to Cary. Offhandedly, I added, "Where's Lindsay?"

"Snowy doesn't want to come in," Cary told me.

"Where's Lindsay?" I asked again, still not overly concerned.

"She's right here," Cary said, looking around. "She was here a minute ago. She followed me from the lake. Maybe she went out again."

Immediately, my antenna went up. "Cary, look to make sure she isn't in the house. Please let me know me as soon as you find her."

Meanwhile, I followed where Snowflake led. Still, no Lindsay. Snowy and I checked the perimeters of our yard, particularly where its borders met two streets. Close neighbors from around the lake saw us outside. When they learned what we were doing they searched for Lindsay with us, to no avail. It was spring and ice in the lake was beginning to melt. We all looked for Lindsay in the adjoining back yards. We looked near the streets. My anxiety was bringing back the same awful emptiness in the pit of my stomach that I felt the first time Lindsay disappeared. I couldn't imagine what I'd do if anything bad happened to our little girl.

It was getting dark when I saw the hole in the ice near the lake shore. Could she have fallen through? By that time neighbors joined the search. I was frantic. So was everyone else. Just as one of the men was preparing to wade into the lake to see if Lindsay had fallen through the ice, a neighbor came running from the house next door. Catching her breath she shouted, "They phoned from the gas station. Lindsay's there."

We drove the half-mile fast to retrieve our child, worried about what we'd find at the filling station. Still panicky, hoping against hope that she'd be alright, we saw her. There was our toddler in the short-order grocery store that was adjacent to the filling station. She was perched on a high stool, gleefully unconcerned about the near riot she'd caused. Lindsay was enraptured by her new friend, the gentle storekeeper. She was eagerly accepting pieces of red licorice that he fed her, bit by bit, from a freshly opened bag in his hand. Obviously, she was having such a happy time that she wasn't at all concerned. After a short while of overwhelming relief, we thanked the friendly storekeeper, scooped Lindsay up and drove her home while she ecstatically clutched the rest of her candy.

I've often wondered about Lindsay's wanderlust. How could she have walked so far from home each time she was lost? I've wondered if she might have been much nearer our house when she wandered, rather than five blocks or half-a-mile away. Could it have been that a kind soul found her wandering aimlessly? Not knowing where she lived, with Lindsay unable to tell them, they may have dropped her where they hoped someone would find her.

We couldn't punish her for running away. She wouldn't have understood. Rather, we blamed ourselves for the times she disappeared in the blink of an eye. Why weren't we more watchful? What means of safety had we overlooked? The only one that was unconcerned was Lindsay. She'd look at us as if to say, "Why would you worry about me? I was just having fun."

Despite those terrifying challenges of her progress, I was pleased that Lindsay was proving the worst predictions wrong. Within her limitations, she improved with each succeeding year.

The only downside was that I wished Don appreciated her gains as I did. Instead, he minimized them as meaningless and drew further away from her. His continuing success in the advertising world pervaded his life. Deeply involved in a profession that included extended out-of-town production trips, entertaining clients and receptions, Don's drinking increased. It worried me, for by that year a third baby was on its way.

"Y...Because We Like You"

At five years old, Lindsay trundled through day after day in happy innocence. She didn't know she had any problems. No one told her. Unsinkable, she breezed along in her own blissful way. Though Lindsay rarely spoke, she refused to be overlooked. A happy child, she danced around the house to the music of the radio or phonograph. She planted herself in the midst of every activity.

Beginning with Bruce's birth three years earlier, one or another of the children occupied every minute of mine except for each afternoon at four o'clock. At that sacred hour, all three dropped whatever they were doing and gathered in a semi-circle in front of the television set. In speechless awe, they watched the Mickey Mouse Club. The only peep out of them for a half-hour was their echo of the Mouseketeers' song, "We're a happy fam...il...ee..." or "Y...because we *like* you!" In her own lisp, Lindsay tried hard to repeat "Y....because we *like* you."

She was such a fan that she wore her adored mouse cap until the black felt ears became so soft they no longer stood up. They flopped around her face and bounced when she walked. She was loath to give up her ears. They went to bed with her at night. They were her badge of belonging to what was happening around her. She loved sharing whatever was happening with her sister, brother and other children.

After school, Cary often brought friends with her for cookies and milk. Lindsay toddled right along after them. Usually she was paces behind but no one cared, least of all Lindsay. She kept up as best she could. Cary, or one of the other girls, would take her hand to help her catch up to the group. Ultimately, her spunk and cheerfulness won everyone over.

But Lindsay was developing challenges that had to be conquered. Her eyes had difficulty focusing. Soon she might need glasses. Her tiny hands shook with tremors, particularly when she was excited. Her coordination was haphazard. She climbed stairs as a baby would, clinging to the banister, then placing both feet on a stair before one foot moved up to the next stair.

No palliative was suggested for my daughter's disabilities. Drugs called tranquilizers remained unknown to me and to the general public, until one morning I received a phone call from a man who introduced himself as Dr. Peterson. He had a pleasant voice and an easy manner. Quickly to the point, he said, "I'm working with a Swiss company on a new drug." I listened as he continued. "We are considering children to participate in an experimental testing program. Your name was referred to us."

I asked him a few questions about who referred me. It was someone I knew and trusted. He went on to ask, "Would you be interested in learning more about the program?" I told him I'd be very interested if the medication could help Lindsay.

"I'd like to go over the details with you and meet Lindsay," he said. We made an appointment for the following week in his office. The day we met, my confidence in Dr. Peterson grew. He gave a detailed explanation of the experimental program. He mentioned that timely reports would be involved along with follow-up appointments. The program seemed worthwhile and I liked his gentle manner with Lindsay. I decided we'd participate for a trial period. The only benefit the doctor didn't divulge was the anticipated result of the drug. When he asked if I minded his giving Lindsay her first pill then and there, his unexpected suggestion gave me pause. He assured me that the medication would do no harm, but he wanted me to tell him what I observed. He

"Will I Be on Television?"

wanted me to learn the result directly from Lindsay's reaction, rather than having him talk about what to look for. Lindsay, ever the eager little soul, took the pill with a cup of water and didn't hesitate for a minute.

After leaving Dr. Peterson's office with a vial of pills, dosage instructions and forms for my first report, we went directly home. I fully expected it would take at least a week, maybe a month, for results. I gave that first small pill no second thought. Not more than three hours later I was amazed at what I saw.

I could hardly believe the impressive decrease in Lindsay's hand tremors. They nearly disappeared. Her eyes were maintaining their focus and, most surprising of all, was her improved coordination. My daughter walked up stairs one at a time as an adult would do. To make sure I was not imagining these improvements, I sat with Lindsay on the stairs and watched her closely. I had her climb up and down a few stairs time and again. My observations were accurate. There was no denying these astounding changes. I went to the phone and called Dr. Peterson. I couldn't wait to share our amazing news.

Soon the Swiss company's name would become recognized in the United States. The family of tranquilizing drugs would be widely used and not only for mental disabilities. My understanding was that in my daughter's case, the drug tranquilized the damaged part of her brain so the undamaged area would strengthen and take over. That accounted for Lindsay's improvement.

This drug marked the beginning of families of drugs for mental disabilities. Lindsay was one of the early beneficiaries. That experimental drug tempered her disabilities, improved her progress and from that day on it became an important factor in her well-being.

At five years, Lindsay was still saying a very few words. She had a little girl lisp. When she began to talk, later than most, she skipped the Mommy and Daddy phase and mimicked more useful words when she heard them used. For example I'd say "dinner's ready." Lindsay would repeat, "dirty woddie," an expression that Cary and Bruce adopted with great glee. After that, dinner was never "ready." "Dirty woddie" was the call to the table. Hearing it as an adult, Lindsay says, "Now you've got me laughing."

I'd say "it's your bed time," and she'd repeat, "bedtime," running the words together. Calling for her sister and brother, she'd lisp, "Cawy" and "Boosh." Even so, with her limited vocabulary, she managed to make her wants known.

To encourage her progress I read children's books aloud, urging her to repeat the sentences. Afternoons we'd have story time. Soon Lindsay picked out the book she wanted read. We rarely finished more than a few pages. But it didn't seem to matter to her. Little by little Lindsay put more words together, particularly when it seemed imperative. Such as, "Boosh is teasing me." Of course, her lisp led to the other two mimicking her. Cary would say, "Mom, Boosh is teasing Lindsay. When I attempted to calm the fray, all three ended up giggling.

Encouragement can be the key to a child's self-confidence and a sense of well-being, especially for the disabled. Throughout Lindsay's life this has been true. Whether living at home or away, she was always encouraged and included as an important participating member of the family.

Following her crisis and her diagnosis, she required special attention. Despite that she couldn't catch up, her siblings constantly included her in their amusements during her toddler years. Lindsay enjoyed the fun even if it was teasing. Somehow, she managed to put the brakes on the other two when necessary. This camaraderie played a major role in her development. The three, all born within five years of each other, were like romping, tussling puppies when they were very young. Often our home seemed like a three-ring circus. Being the middle child, Lindsay was given no chance to hang back.

"Will I Be on Television?"

Her older sister treated her as self-sufficient, expecting much of her, but Cary was intuitive when the need arose. She taught and guided Lindsay subtly and tenderly. Bruce, her younger brother, always looking for a playmate, pummeled, prodded and was the tease. But sensing Lindsay's fragility, Bruce never carried the roughness too far. Lindsay became adept at holding her own. A deep unspoken bond thrived among the three, built on a foundation of love, understanding and a mutual sense of humor. There was no sibling rivalry. When Cary and Bruce got into trouble their overworked chant to me was, of course, "Lindsay made us do it."

My next effort to help Lindsay cope with the world we lived in began by thinking ahead. Considering that her eventual education would be in the public school system, I believed a head start before kindergarten would be helpful. Nursery schools, still in their infancy, seemed the best place to begin. Generally, children at four or five were enrolled. Because of Lindsay's slower development it seemed wiser to hold her back a year. She was still tiny. Even at six years she would fit in stature with the other younger children. In those days, nursery schools followed public schools' schedules, starting school in fall, closing in spring. Just after spring closing, the year Lindsay would enroll, I called the teacher of Cary's pre-school. We'd become friends when Cary was a student. The well-regarded school served compatible families, likely to understand Lindsay's situation. The teacher suggested we meet at the school, where Lindsay immediately made herself at home in the classroom and with the toys. Including Lindsay in the class was an experiment. We agreed to begin with half-days until it was certain that she was accepted by the other children.

Lindsay needed no encouragement to join with the group. But she needed extra help when a new activity was begun. Patient and kind, the teacher encouraged her to try new skills. My daughter was still behind the other youngsters in her development so the wise teacher allowed her to learn at her own pace. She was accepted by the other children who were too young to question her slower progress. They became friends and she found her place in the class.

My irrepressible five-year-old participated enthusiastically. She loved the singing and dancing she was taught. It was a way for her to belong and perform. Gaily responding to the music she heard in school and at home, our tiny tyke sailed through life with her usual bounce, a twirl and a smile. But she did not catch up to the other children in learned skills. It was obvious. Her teacher and I met several times to determine what was best to do next for Lindsay's education. My head start idea hadn't borne the fruit we hoped it would. The question we mulled over was *should Lindsay try kindergarten or should we keep her home?* Separate classes for children with special needs were non-existent in public schools. Lindsay would be with typical children in the kindergarten class. That was the problem. But it seemed better than being home all day without being taught. All things considered, Lindsay's attempting kindergarten won. "Let's give it a try," we mutually decided.

During a conversation at the nursery school one of the mothers told me, "Children don't have to be cookie-cutter replicas to have friends." I brightened at her understanding of my daughter's impairment. I was sincerely touched by her kindness.

What I didn't know during that conversation was that my plan to have Lindsay begin in pre-kindergarten would be a harbinger of experimental *mingling* in a Southern city many years later. As colleges began to offer courses in Special Education for teachers, forerunner programs resulted. Introducing children with special needs into the regular pre-kindergarten population was one of them. Its importance is having these children together with typical children at the earliest ages. Not only does this *mingling* promote acceptance of the mentally-impaired by other youngsters, the young children vie to help those with disabilities. As a result, the typical children have an understanding and a special bond with the disabled. No longer experimental, but proven beneficial, a number of such pre-schools sprouted across the country. The number remains too small. Waiting lists are long, not only for the challenged, but also for average and bright children whose parents understand the range of benefits these schools offer. I'm reminded of Lindsay's Nursery School playmate's mother who believed that all children are valuable, despite their differences.

I wondered, at the time, how would my child have fared without this private nursery school support? Would a public institution have provided the same chance to participate? What happens to children whose parents who can't afford these resources? In the fifties, support specifically earmarked for the mentally challenged was rare to non-existent.

During Lindsay's lifetime there have been worthwhile changes. Attitudes toward the disabled improved significantly. Government and privately-sponsored organizations offer helpful solutions for many problems. Still more is needed. It remains necessary to find information and aid for each individual situation. As my daughter grew, we were fortunate in discovering how to do so.

"They Pushed Me"

Following Lindsay's head start of two years in nursery school, I had high hopes for her. Kindergarten would be her first venture into the real world. If she could keep up with the other youngsters, she might be able to do well in the next elementary school grades.

It was important for Lindsay to succeed, for in 1959 the fate of children with developmental disabilities was dim. In the 1800s a crusading woman, Dorothea Dix, recognized one vital need. By pursuing the legislature, she achieved a law to correct deplorable conditions in institutional housing for the afflicted. But not all institutions were improved. In the fifties many were still dreadful. State institutions were for those identified as mentally retarded, schizophrenic, or by the catch-all phrase, demented. Homes for almost 200,000, provided only minimal food, clothing and shelter, but no education.

Not until the 1960s was the first definition of "developmentally-disabled" written. When Lindsay began kindergarten, few schools had specifically trained teachers. Special education was rare. Tutors were unavailable. As long as my daughter lived at home, public school classes were the only option for her education and they were scarce

―◆・I・◆・―

At six, Lindsay already faced serious challenges. She'd be the oldest in her class, but being small should help her fit in. Glasses made her look different. Though socially she was eager, she rarely began a conversation or continued one. When we spoke to her she'd repeat one or two of the words she heard. Mostly, she'd reply with only a few words. Or she'd answer with the same word we'd used. If I'd say, "It's time for lunch," Lindsay would say, "lunch." If Cary or Bruce would say, "Let's play hide-and-seek," Lindsay would say either "play" or "hide," or "seek." We understood and made allowances for her, but would teachers and other children?

In an attempt to help her deal with these problems, we created games. Cary and I cut poster board into rectangular flash cards. We drew simple pictures on them and wrote matching words in large print. CAT, DOG and HOUSE were a few of the words we chose. Cary would hold up a card and point to the picture. "House," she'd say. "Housh," mimicked Lindsay, grinning happily and pointing to the picture. With her little girl lisp, she'd repeat whatever word she heard. We'd use the word in a short sentence, teaching her to repeat, "It's my house." She loved the game.

When we weren't working with her, she'd sit on the carpet, gather the cards around her, mix them up and study each individually. Or she'd bring a stack to one of us, so we'd play the game with her. I couldn't be sure how much she understood. I hoped the word association would help her learn.

As usual, Cary was the 'little mother,' preparing her sister for a new adventure. She told Lindsay, "Kindergarten is just like nursery school, but there will be more children. You'll make new friends and have exciting things to do. You'll paint pictures just like you do with Aunt Betty." We also tried to anticipate what might frighten Lindsay, unexpected bells or being bumped in the hallways. We hoped our explanations would ease whatever apprehension she might feel. The more often we talked about school, the more she seemed to understand.

Particularly, I wanted to put a good face on Lindsay's handling the new challenges she'd have to face without help. "You'll be just fine," I told her frequently. I'd say, "You'll love riding in the

"Will I Be on Television?"

big yellow school bus," or, "Your teacher will be very nice to you." While we could never be sure of Lindsay's understanding, she was looking forward to her first day. She was excited. We knew she'd try to do her best.

To further pave the way for our daughter and prepare the school staff for what might be her special needs, I requested a conference. Despite busy schedules, the principal and teacher were willing and accommodating.

"Lindsay will be eager to keep up," I explained at the meeting, "But there are simple tasks that might be hard for her." I'd made a list of the areas that caused her difficulties and gave them the list. "She's used to having decisions made for her. She's happy to cooperate with them," I told them. "But there may be times she'll need assistance." They said they were willing to work with her. It was easy to see that they wanted her to succeed. "We'll do everything we can to help," they both told me. Reassured by their understanding, I felt convinced that Lindsay would receive beginning training and a foundation for her continuing education.

My concern was that she had never before encountered a challenge without one of her family standing by. She'd never known anything but support and kindness. The staff didn't tell me that Lindsay would be the only mentally-disabled youngster in the school. She would face this new experience entirely alone.

The first day of school, my eager daughter was excited when I lifted her onto the high step of the school bus. She managed the next two steps by herself and happily climbed aboard her seat. I waved at the bus as it departed, but by that time she was too engrossed to look out the window. I had every reason to be as excited as Lindsay. I hoped with all my heart that all would go well.

As the hours moved along, I turned into a clock-watcher, marking time until she returned. I was hardly able to wait to learn about her day. My hopes soared as I watched the school bus round a corner near our home. But as I helped her clamor down from the steps, those hopes crashed. Lindsay's face was tear-stained, her knees were skinned and her new dress was torn. Could she have fallen? Was she badly hurt?

Bewildered, she flew into my arms. With tears dripping down her cheeks, she cried, "They pushed me." Apparently, she'd been mistreated. She couldn't say more than, "They pushed me." She didn't understand why. It broke my heart. In the house, I hoped to soothe her while I treated her scrapes and bruises. That plucky little soul winced and almost cried again when I dabbed at her cuts with stinging Mercurochrome. Instead, with watery eyes, she blubbered, "I'm brave."

Later, her teacher told me that Lindsay was pushed off the swings and merry-go-round when she tried to join the other youngster's play during recess. "She kept up rather well with the other children in her class," the teacher said. "It wasn't the kindergartners who bothered her on the playground. It was the older students.

"They realized she was mentally-impaired and made fun of her. I saw the teasing too late to prevent her being hurt," the teacher apologized. She said the playground was gravel. The stones could be sharp. She'd kept Lindsay with her until it was time to go home.

Lindsay didn't want to go back to school. I couldn't blame her. Her first day was too much of a shock. She was too trusting and innocent to understand why she was teased and hurt. Still, since the only alternative was for her to be home all day, we had to try school at least once more. The principal agreed. More than one afternoon was needed for Lindsay to become less fearful and to determine if the other children would behave. We decided we'd give the situation a few days' rest, then try again.

Lindsay would be safe in the regular class, but during recess, after school and on the bus, our concern was that anyone differ-

"Will I Be on Television?"

ent stood out as a target. Could the other children change their ways without understanding the importance of doing so? Or would Lindsay be mocked, ridiculed or hurt again? The faculty was extremely troubled by these actions and corrected problems as they arose. But teachers couldn't be everywhere. Some children found nothing wrong with their humiliating behavior.

It was hard for Lindsay to face the challenge alone. Had Cary attended the same grammar school, Lindsay would have had a protector. But Cary was enrolled in a different school that recently had been built for the advanced grades.

We talked with Lindsay about trying school again. Clearly, she was afraid. Even though I told my daughter I'd take her to school and stay with her until she was safely in her classroom, she was still frightened. Nevertheless, we talked her into trying again. She agreed, although hesitantly. It was a decision that marked the beginning of her future courage. That day I recognized what a trouper my little daughter could be.

My mind wasn't at ease a week later when she was willing to try again, so I drove her to school. As our car pulled up to front of the building, I noticed a group of older boys idling on the walk leading to the main door. Several of them watched us get out of the car. When they saw Lindsay, two started to mimic her, exaggerating her slow responses while others laughed. I felt an ache of sadness and hoped Lindsay didn't understand. When the boys saw my anger they turned away and escaped into the building.

With misgivings, I walked with Lindsay to her classroom. I told her teacher about the boys' teasing and understood she'd look into the problem. We also talked of recess and whether I should plan to pick my daughter up after school. Lindsay's teacher promised, "I'll watch over her during recess. We should try the school bus again, and I'll alert the bus driver."

I hoped her concern was enough to protect Lindsay. It was very hard for me to leave my trusting child alone in the uncertain situation, but I knew I had to do it. It was the only way for Lindsay to succeed in public school.

That afternoon I met her bus again. She seemed edgy, though she couldn't tell me what bothered her. When Cary came home, Lindsay began to relax and enjoy their playing together. During the rest of the week, there were no other incidents. Although Lindsay was never eager to leave for kindergarten, she seemed less fearful. This continued for two days into the following week. I believed the situation was improving. She didn't talk about being bothered by other children. I, too, began to relax.

But the third day she came home crying. Her sweater was torn. Apparently, some of the other students' behavior wasn't going to change. Seeing that Lindsay had been teased again, handled roughly and had her feelings trampled on, I was more heartbroken than Lindsay. I realized I'd made a huge mistake by sending her to public school. I refused to subject her to being an outcast ever again. I made the decision not send her back to kindergarten. The school staff understood and agreed. Children's teasing each other has been timeless, but "bullying" as a modern problem has become terrifying. It has grown to gangs bent on destroying others. In one publicized case it lead to a young girl's suicide.

Though I had no idea how to find other means of educating of my daughter, I was determined to try. For Lindsay to live at home and be taught might necessitate a move to another city. I had no way of knowing if that would be necessary. At the time there were no resources for learning about available education for children with special needs in our city or anywhere else. For our family a move was problematic for too many reasons. Don would be unwilling to leave his job and increasing success. I couldn't expect that of him. My other children would leave excellent schools. To sell our recently built home would mean financial loss. We were

"Will I Be on Television?"

comfortable in our suburban neighborhood. There seemed no way to resolve our dilemma.

It wasn't until 1975, when Congress enacted the *Education for All Handicapped Children Act,* that public schools began to offer Special Education classes on a regular basis. Specialists were being taught to train the disabled. In the fifties I didn't know that by 1975 I would be trained in social work. I would learn where and how to seek help. But in the fifties, when my daughter needed help desperately, I was flying blind with no idea how or where to start searching.

Lindsay still couldn't grasp many tasks of daily living, shoelaces, her hair, difficult buttons, organizing her clothes. I tried teaching her myself. We spent more time together. At times we paged through books, tried simple writing and played with educational toys. But I soon discovered I wasn't a good instructor. I was too emotionally involved to help her learn. Rather than watch her struggle time and again, I would do whatever was necessary for her. Or I'd concentrate on having her improve the simple tasks she'd already accomplished. Though we got along quite well, Lindsay wasn't progressing. She wasn't learning the elementary skills she'd need for the rest of her life.

What I didn't recognize at the time were unexpected benefits. Although Lindsay wasn't up to her age level in daily living requirements, or making intellectual gains, she developed in other ways. Betty devoted more time to Lindsay. Her loving devotion, her understanding and attention, encouraged my daughter's emotional growth. Betty would have been an outstanding teacher of all children. It became apparent as she entertained Lindsay with stories, books, music and teaching her the joy of painting, one or two mornings each week.

Lindsay's siblings contributed to her future well-being in ways we didn't realize at the time and that we've laughed about many times since. On the one hand she profited from Cary's mothering and imagination, while on the other hand she was the elected recipient of her little brother Bruce's boyish roughhousing. She protected herself with a series of war cries if he became too rough. For her long-range benefit, Cary's and Bruce's creative antics kept her actively engaged and increased her self-confidence.

Much to Lindsay's delight, Cary invented SHPs just for her. Together, the two would wander an unknown distance from our house, not to be heard from for an hour or more. Although they were out of sight, I never worried. Our neighborhood was small and safe. Those days we didn't lock our doors. We weren't wary of strangers. Returning home giggling, Cary'd whisper "shush!" in Lindsay's ear and Lindsay would repeat, "shush!" I wondered why their clothing held a few scattered leaves and small twigs. Since they couldn't go far and returned happy and laughing, I didn't pry into their secret. Years later, Cary told me, "SHP stands for Secret Hiding Places." They would tumble into gulleys and under bushes, certain they were hidden from probing eyes. The two little girls were small enough to imagine that the bushes were forests with foliage high over their heads and the gulleys were deep ravines. Cary created the game just for Lindsay, who loved it. Only subtly did I question Cary about what the girls did. Their secrets tickled them so and they were harmless.

When Bruce played with Lindsay, my antenna went up immediately. Bruce liked to wrestle and Lindsay needed a defender. Bruce was too young to understand that an opponent could be hurt and Lindsay was frequently the nearest sacrificial lamb. Fortunately, Bruce was too little to do harm and Lindsay's ability at self-protection could make him behave. "Boosh is teasing me," she'd call for my help. Or "Boosh is sitting on me." One of her best was "Boosh is anxious!" Lindsay's vocabulary for words she heard us use became some of our favorites. For instance, "anxious" replaced "obnoxious" in our family's personal dictionary for years.

"Will I Be on Television?"

It was when Cary and Bruce got together to urge Lindsay into some devilish prank that my temperature rose. One episode was the time I was out in the yard for a chat with a neighbor that took longer than expected. I was greeted as I walked back into the house by, *"Mom, Lindsay smoked!"* Scattered on the carpet were torn bits of my cigarettes and broken matches. It took me a few minutes of being stunned to realize that none of the cigarettes had burned ends and none of the broken matches had been lighted. My relief must have been striking. The children's giggles—Lindsay's included—increased throughout the day. For years we've laughed about *"Mom, Lindsay smoked."*

Whatever the children were up to included their sister. They paid no attention to her disability, compensating without thought for what she couldn't do. She'd be hidden for their hide-and-seek games and found before she became frightened. She'd wear the funny hats and help blow out candles at birthday parties. She joined them playing with Snowflake's puppies. For her birthday, we became a four-person team spending a full day shopping for the pet parakeet she named Mikey, that the other two would care for. Lindsay was never left behind.

In retrospect, the year that Lindsay remained home from public school may have played a large part in laying the foundation for what later would be termed her 'emotional intelligence.' Different skills can compensate for intellectual disabilities. Lindsay developed many. Some were fostered by experiences in early childhood. She learned other skills from happy and silly times with her sister and brother that continued from childhood throughout her life. They provided a strong base for the personality, self-confidence and sense of humor that has served her well through the years.

"Where is Daddy?"

Something awful was happening within our small family. What was it? I hadn't a clue. At first the changes were so gradual I convinced myself that any problem must be my imagination. Still, more and more of Don's actions were not like him. "I'll be back soon," he'd tell me, surprising me by taking the car out on a family Sunday afternoon for no reason and with no explanation. When he'd return several hours later, the rest of the day was no different from other Sundays. He'd unbutton the top buttons of his shirt, roll up his sleeves, slide off his shoes and prop his stocking feet on the footstool of his Daddy chair in the living room.

Cary would eagerly climb on his lap. Together they'd read the Funny Papers, laughing about favorite cartoons, Popeye, Mandrake the Magician, Maggie and Jiggs. I'd spend time with Lindsay, encouraging her physical prowess or playing games that helped her mentally. If Don returned later than usual, I'd be in the kitchen making dinner. That he offered no explanation for his sudden departures was puzzling but I was too busy to worry about them.

His weekday schedule, home at six o'clock without fail, was revised some evenings. "I'll be late," he'd phone. "Busy," he'd say. For the longest time that didn't surprise me. With Don's increasing success his job was bound to become more demanding. His tardiness was easy to understand, until I learned his ad agency's office closed at 5:30 sharp. More nights he'd arrive home at eight or nine o'clock. I ignored whatever was the truth because I wasn't looking for a problem. If there was one, I believed it had something to do with his work and I didn't fancy the role of henpecking wife.

Though I learned that *seventy-five percent of marriages with handicapped children ended in divorce*, I had no reason to believe that statistic could apply to Don's and my marriage. Divorce never entered my mind. No one in my family divorced. None among our married friends divorced. For me, divorce held no place in "polite society." I felt secure about our marriage and was certain that Don felt the same. Nevertheless, I began to worry about what I didn't know. Living with questions, at times suspicions, became harder and harder to bear.

As Don's withdrawal from our family was more obvious, I tried to accept it. Because of the demands on my time, household chores, three children and devoting extra attention to Lindsay's particular needs, I saw no other option. Not only was my time required for daily living tasks, it also was necessary to take Lindsay to psychological and medical appointments. Don's lack of interest in those appointments was particularly conspicuous. His interaction with Lindsay was non-existent. He used every excuse to avoid the help with her that I asked for frequently. Still, I couldn't foresee that Don's changing behavior would result in a permanent catastrophe for the children and me. I believed we'd work through this rough patch, whatever it was.

Don and I had every basis for a lasting marriage. We'd had a four-year courtship that led to the unforgettable night we attended a fraternity dinner dance. Surrounded by friends orchestrating the traditional ceremony, Don attached his fraternity pin to my dress near my heart. Our storybook wedding in one of Milwaukee's most imposing hallowed churches included the traditional complement of bridesmaids, grooms-men, guests and *until us death do us part* vows. I trusted those vows and was certain Don did, too. We were in love and looked forward to a long life together "for better or worse."

"Will I Be on Television?"

Eighteen months later, while Cary was still a small baby, Don faced an unplanned recall of Air Force Reserve officers for the Korean War. After his lengthy service as a B52 bomber's navigator in WWII, he deeply resented this added tour. The first weekend after he reported for duty, I heard a knock on our apartment door and opened it to see my husband standing there in full uniform looking strikingly handsome. Thrilled and in his arms I blurted, "How did you manage this?"

"I'm AWOL," he said. I was too happy to question his answer and never learned whether he was telling the truth or joking. The moodiness and depression that followed him for the rest of the years of his service began three days later when he had to return to his base. As he was leaving us that Sunday he begged me to follow him with Cary, as soon as possible. I packed up what was in our apartment and put it in storage. In the bright red convertible he bought with his additional pay, Cary and I drove cross-country to join him only a few weeks later.

Don was often depressed during those next years in the Air Force. I found it hard to understand. No matter how I tried to encourage some enjoyment of where we were and what we did, he couldn't rid himself of his anger. He resented being where he didn't want to be and doing what he didn't want to do. He feared being sent overseas. What he wanted was to be back in the world of the advertising business and safe from war. Help came to me through coincidence. As an officer's wife, with the background of a psychology minor in college, I volunteered as a uniformed Gray Lady at the local veteran's hospital. I worked with returned veterans helping them cope with traumatic stress. The coincidence for Don was my friendship with a staff psychiatrist who taught me how to help allay my husband's depression and fears.

Though his deep-down anger and fear never left Don entirely, with love and some travel away from the base for extra training, the three years of his service passed with only one instance of serious concern. He refused to fly overseas with his group. This caused him to be officially reprimanded and shunned by the men on the base. It depressed him further. So, it was a welcome change to see how his discharge and our return home snapped him out of his personality change almost overnight.

As he had hoped, the advertising agency job he loved had been held for him while he was away. With a substantial increase in income, we successfully clambered over the hurdle of living from paycheck to paycheck with children. Our oldest daughter, then three, was a charmer. Lindsay was on-the-way soon after and as those checks increased we bought a small bungalow. Eventually, a rambunctious baby boy was ours. For extra roominess we built a new home on a lake. Life for a couple in their late twenties should have been one of perfect contentment. In fact, contentment favored us for many years, until two dramatic happenings clashed head on and forever altered our future.

The first event was thrilling. Don and his creative artist partner at the advertising agency originated a beer commercial for television that made them nationally famous. Almost overnight my husband's life became a sunburst. He was lauded in the advertising world and in public. Trips to Hollywood to work on new commercials became the norm. We entertained famous show folks in our home. We mounted a whirlwind of excitement and splendor.

The second event, though, wrested much of the wind from those full sails. Lindsay was diagnosed as "mentally retarded" and it became more apparent that she would never have the life of a typical child. As Don's activities were transformed, mine were too. Experience with Lindsay's lack of both physical and mental growth, while finding only evasive medical answers to my questions, forced some acknowledgement that our daughter might never be an independent child or adult. Most disturbing was that the information we were given was not enough to learn what we could do to help her.

"Will I Be on Television?"

Without realizing it was happening, Don and I were drawn in two diametrically opposite directions. During the fifties suburban men concentrated overtime on success in their careers. Wives were homemakers and mothers. It was a fine arrangement as long as it was balanced. But we lost our balance along the way.

As Don rode his wave of success, I grappled with poignant grief and fruitless attempts to *make lemonade from the lemons* that clung to our adorable second daughter. I was intractable in defying the doctors' and some of Don's family members' advice to put Lindsay in an institution. Don's grandmother never accepted her great granddaughter. In those years, families who had "retarded" children were brutally stigmatized and the stigma of having a "retarded" child spread to the extended family.

For two years I was certain Lindsay would recover from her frightening second morning in the hospital. Though she'd been stiff, motionless and entirely unresponsive in my arms it took longer than two years for me to accept the truth of her disability.

I remembered too well the afternoon Lindsay was hospitalized. I'd been able to restore her breathing after her very close call. When I left her in the security of the hospital's care she was the baby I knew. So, despite her being so unlike herself that second morning, I was convinced that the damage to her couldn't be permanent. When she was discharged two days later she had seemingly recovered. She no longer had the symptoms of that second morning. The only difference I'd noticed was that she wasn't holding her head up as strongly as she had before her frightening incident.

In retrospect, it was emotion and denial that made me postpone the truth of Lindsay's handicap. Still, I've always been grateful that my denial ended shortly after Lindsay's earliest two years. I was able to acknowledge the seriousness of her problem before my delay in finding the right kind of help would cause her a setback. Her first two years were consumed with doctors' and psychologists' appointments, in an attempt to seek an exact diagnosis, prognosis and help. In the 50s that was not an easy task. I wasn't the only one who didn't acknowledge the severity of my daughter's disability. The medical group I hoped to learn from was very close-mouthed. I tried, but I couldn't draw out the answers I searched for what would apply to Lindsay's care and future. Our pediatrician regularly pulled back from telling me the truth when I asked about Lindsay's slower development. He'd beg the question saying, "I see no change." Don's and my time together suffered as a result of my pre-occupation with Lindsay. No longer could he use me for the role of sounding board for his creative ideas. There were too many distractions and interruptions.

When I needed a strong shoulder to lean on, Don's shoulder wasn't offered. Lindsay and I received no support from her father whom I believed should be as concerned about her as I was. And I needed his determination to match mine in the struggle to prevent our daughter from being sentenced to life in some horrible institution.

True to Don's Scandinavian upbringing, he rarely shared his innermost emotions. Did he grieve about Lindsay as I did? I never knew. He didn't offer an opinion about institutionalizing her. Did he encourage or discourage Lindsay's remaining at home? If I tried to tell him what I'd learned about a positive future for our child, he'd change the subject or walk away. If I'd ask for a decision, he'd dodge the issue. The dilemma of our daughter's future remained unresolved. He was as disinterested in Lindsay as if she wasn't there. With Bruce, he would become furiously angry for no reason. Bruce was still a toddler and mischievous.

My husband's drinking increased markedly. I protected our children as much as I could and wondered if his aggravation with them might be the result of his demanding job. At the time he was wrapped up in making his mark in the advertising world.

Night after night, I'd make excuses when my husband missed dinner and sometimes arrived home at two or three in the morning. He'd phone to say, "We're working late," and often phone more than once to extend his arrival time. Sometimes I'd hear music in the background. When Cary asked me, "Where's Daddy?" my usual answer was, "Daddy has to work overtime." I'd make up other excuses as well. For a while I believed my excuses, though I realized our problems were growing. Because extra time was required for Lindsay's care and for our other two children who also needed my time and attention, I found it difficult to cope with Don's behavior. His success might have made life easier. Instead, our lives were moving fast in the opposite direction.

Don traveled to Hollywood frequently. The first time we went together and had a wonderful time, but he never included me again. Following several trips he showed me a catalog of starlets, seeking my opinion about which one was most attractive for a commercial he planned. His trip, immediately after, was suspiciously extended.

He'd been away for a long two weeks. Cary missed him, so when we expected him home from that journey, I asked the three children, "Would you like to meet Daddy at his plane?" Their excited answers left no question. They loved to watch the planes take off and land. Scrubbed and dressed they eagerly scrambled into the car. Their excitement had us laughing and singing all the way to the airport. They tumbled out, almost one over another, in the parking lot. After watching other planes for some time, we saw Don's plane arrive. It didn't take long for their fast-moving Daddy, jacket over his arm and briefcase in hand, to stride toward us down the walkway. He was engrossed in conversation with several men and didn't see us immediately. I held back the three to keep them from charging as he approached. When he was quite near, they rushed to hug him. His expression erupted in fury. "I'll see you at home," he said, brushing off his heartbroken children who didn't understand. He strode on with his companions.

As I was forced to face the change in Don, it was obvious that a wife and three small children, particularly one who was *different*, didn't fit the image he wished to project to the public.

"Grass Soup"

At the time our third child was conceived Don didn't want another baby. He may have feared that another child might have a problem or he may not have wanted an additional responsibility that would be an unbreakable tie to family life. He didn't say. What he did tell me was that he wanted me to ask my obstetrician for an abortion. Quite a few things Don did caused me to suspect he'd prefer to be a bachelor again.

"Don't be concerned about your new baby," the doctor said when I brought up the subject. "It's early, but everything seems to be progressing well. The embryo is fine and so are you." He asked, "You don't really want an abortion, do you?"

"No," I said, "I don't."

"Why would you consider it?" I told him that my husband wanted it.

"I don't do abortions," he said. His tone was sharp. His words were brusque. "I'll see you in a month. If you have any problems in the meantime, call and make an appointment." He walked out the door of the examining room without another word.

Don wasn't happy about the outcome of our consultation. But nature took its course and Bruce began his life as a perfect baby boy, strong, healthy, with an immediate mind of his own. Even as a toddler, Bruce loved to climb. I'd find him in unexpected places, never knowing what mind set propelled him. I was amazed that he was so agile for I had to rescue him frequently.

Jan Amis Jessup

At four years, one very early morning Bruce decided on a particularly creative plan. I'm not sure what awakened me early that morning at 2:00 a.m. It must have been the light from our family room shining down the long dark hall to our bedroom. I moved slowly, not really wanting to be awake and certainly not wanting to get up in what was the middle of the night. Don was asleep. The thought of a burglar entered my mind. I pushed it away and didn't awaken him.

Groping my way toward our family room in the darkness, the first thing I saw were piles of used celluloid movie tape, tangled and scattered from one side of the room to the other. The movie camera was half-hidden in the pile. Then I saw Bruce, in his pajamas not in the family room. In the kitchen beyond, he was perched precariously on a chair pulled over from the breakfast area to the edge of the built in burner plate of the stove. He was leaning over a burner with his small hand on the handle of a sauce pan. The pan, empty of water held an egg still in its shell.

I was aghast! Bruce could have burned himself badly. He could have set fire to the house. Thank goodness, I saw that he hadn't turned on the electric burner. As I'd hoped when I saw him, he hadn't learned how. Innocently, he was waiting for me to praise him. "I'm making breakfast," he bragged. "I'm going to watch a movie."

Another time our adventurous son terrified a baby-sitter and me. Bruce was not fond of being left behind when I was away from home. Nevertheless, I drove off in our convertible certain that all was well with the baby-sitter and for my three children. More than a mile from home I heard a wee, easily recognized, voice behind me say, "Hi Mom." I couldn't turn my head to see Bruce. I had to watch the road. I came near to slamming on the brake. Fortunately, there was an empty space to pull the car to the curb. Bruce's eyes peered at me from over the top of the deep well behind the front seat that held the car's fabric top when it was lowered.

"Hi Mom," the wee stowaway said once more with a grin I could picture before I saw it. My meeting was forgotten. Bruce and I rushed home to calm a terrified baby-sitter who was searching all over the house for him. To this day I wonder how he climbed into the car, closed the car door behind himself and wriggled into that very tight well.

Alerting me to another very serious problem, neighbors mentioned seeing Bruce play with lighted matches in our back yard. They were aware of Don's absentee fathering and they worried about our son. Bruce had no mentor to guide him. Our next-door neighbor stepped in gracefully to fill Don's role. He spent many hours at his grill in the back yard, teaching Bruce how to light fires carefully and to respect their danger.

Those neighbors, and others, saw that the destruction of our family was taking its toll on the children. Desperately, I wanted to believe that Don would eventually respect the responsibilities he'd helped create and return to being the husband and father I knew. I believed in him though friends of ours also were making derogatory remarks about his behavior.

Hinting, some joked about "three Martini lunches in the advertising game." They used humor to disguise their concerns. Don had been only a beer drinker so I didn't immediately realize they meant my husband. Alcoholism captures its victims subtly.

As our life together deteriorated, I sought counseling. That was when I was shown the statistic that seventy-five percent of marriages with children having special needs ended in divorce. I tried to put that statistic out of my mind. I feared divorce for many reasons. First among them was that I feared for my children. Children need a father figure. Bruce, particularly, needed his father. Despite that Don was over-bearing and I saw him be mean to his son, Bruce tagged after him. I could see the hurt in Bruce's expression when he was reprimanded for no reason, or brushed off. He was feeling the pain of the family break-up. My over-arching goal was to protect my children.

Don attended our first counseling session and wouldn't continue. I followed up for I still hoped to save our family. Phyllis, the counselor was perceptive. She described Don by saying, "He grew up in a cotton batting world." Over-protected as a boy he couldn't face problems or take responsibility. She said, "He avoids problems if possible." We talked about his personality change during the Korean War. "This is the same," she said. "But this is more complicated because of his increasing drinking."

Family birthdays were always special events, especially for the children. Lindsay's was approaching and we all wanted Don to join us the Saturday we shopped for her gift. It was to be a pet parakeet. "Can't make it," Don said. "I'm working on a new commercial." Cary begged him several times. She wanted to know, "Why isn't Daddy coming with us?"

At the pet shop all three had a great time watching the puppies and kittens and especially the birds. Cary helped Lindsay choose her favorite bird from a number of parakeets hopping about in an over-sized cage. Cary pointed to a chirping yellow fellow with a bright red cap.

"Mikey," Cary said. "Would you like to name him Mikey?" she asked her sister. Lindsay laughed happily. "Mikey," she said quite clearly.

So, with the cage, stand, bird bath, bird seed and all, Mikey came home with us in a cardboard box with a screened window. Soon, the cage was assembled. It hung high on its stand, reigning in splendor in the middle of our family room. For three minutes!

In a single charging swoop across the room, our usually staid and patient collie leapt at the hanging cage and knocked its bottom to the floor. Our dog scattered the cage's contents, water, bird seed, and a terrified Mikey onto the carpet. The

"Will I Be on Television?"

trembling bird was being tracked by a sniffing dog. On the carpet, on my hands and knees, I managed to save Mikey from Snowflake's tongue. This surprise behavior was so unlike our unusually calm and patient collie that I could hardly believe what I'd just seen.

I took Snowflake by the collar to another room and believed Mikey was safe. But the dog was not to be thwarted. The entire scene repeated itself almost exactly. Except, the second time I wasn't on my hands and knees, I was on my stomach, saving a far more frazzled parakeet. That may have been the day hysteria hatched one of our family's favorite sayings, *when you don't know whether to laugh or cry, laugh!*

After managing to retrieve Mikey and pen Snowflake in the basement, the parakeet finally found a permanently safe home in another room. Mikey's cage was hung where Snowflake couldn't reach it. All afternoon Lindsay watched and studied Mikey, chuckling cheerfully at his every hop. For years, Mikey was Lindsay's beloved member of the family. He lived in a cage in her room near her bed.

By the time we gathered around the table to blow out candles and munch birthday cake, we were all giggling. Cary couldn't wait to describe the *adventure* to her Daddy. But somewhere along the way Don had misplaced his sense of humor. It was just as well that he hadn't been with us. He would have left abruptly during the first catastrophe.

I continued my meetings with Phyllis. "You can tell from the cartoon commercials Don creates that he's still a little boy," she said. Phyllis was the first to recommend divorce. "Protect yourself and the children," she told me. I wondered aloud if Don talked about his feelings toward Lindsay. She couldn't answer because of confidentiality, but after I brought it up she said, "Next time, find a better man."

It was difficult to equate Phyllis's recommendation to divorce my husband with protecting my children. I believed divorce was the worst possible course. I believed that divorce could severely affect not only our children's present well-being, but their entire future outlook on life? Phyllis agreed that it might affect them. She said, "But you may find it's better for them to have a settled life with one parent they can depend on than for them to continue the stressful life they have now." She knew that my children were my most important concern.

I still loved the man I'd shared my life with for more than eleven years. *And I was learning how tragic it was to watch someone I loved in a downward spiral that I was helpless to stop.* I still clung to a measure of hope that Don might realize his need for help and resolve the situation.

Sadly, the outcome was quite different. His addiction became worse. For four years I'd attempted to hold our marriage together. I sought our minister's advice and that of a doctor friend. I sensed that neither of them wanted to be involved in our marital problems. Perhaps they knew us both too well. No possible solutions were offered, not even recommendations. Our minister tried briefly to help but said he didn't feel he knew enough about Don's possible reactions to be of real help. When I described the situation to our doctor his answer was, "The problem is complicated."

Don continued to live at home, but as our son and the girls grew, he became more remote, more aggressive. The trauma of our family breakup was harming us all because I could no longer hide my anguish from the children. Instead, what they needed most was my strength and support.

In desperation, as a final attempt to save our family, I called Alcoholics Anonymous. Though it was a rare occurrence, a member of AA came to our home. Unfortunately, even the member's attempt to work with my husband failed. He suggested divorce. He also said, "If you threaten divorce and it doesn't change your husband's behavior, the only possible ray of hope is to go through with it."

"Will I Be on Television?"

After that conversation I continued attempting to forestall divorce for as long as possible. Don's behavior didn't change. With each passing week I became less able to handle the destruction of our family. A good friend sent a mutual acquaintance to see me. She talked to me about having lived with an alcoholic husband and described the serious problems her teenage children suffered. Shortly after that Don spent one night drinking heavily. When I begged him to stop he left home in a rage. I urged him to come home but he never returned. The combination of the AA member's advice, my concern for my children's futures and Don's desertion, made a decision imperative. I could no longer postpone filing for divorce. Don didn't, or couldn't, veer from the direction he'd chosen. Our divorce became final.

Unless you've been there, you can never know how devastating it is to feel the entire pattern of your life fall apart. We lived in the age of mid-west suburbia. Families were solid. Fathers achieved. Mothers were homemakers who cared for their husband's needs and majored in parenting. We were Sunday school teachers, good cooks and, in whatever spare time we might find, we were volunteers helping those less fortunate.

I was brought up to excel in school, to continue in college and to marry before twenty-five or face being an "*old maid.*" Three children was the norm. Work outside the home was not a badge of honor. The badge of honor was bringing up your children to be independent adults of good character, integrity and with the necessary tools to be successful in their own lives. All of that changed with the divorce. The question was *what do we do now?*

Fortunately, we still had our home. But knowing Don's penchant for high living the wherewithal to remain in it was questionable. With three young children a full time job was impossible. I was naïve and knew so little of the larger world that my outlook for my children's and my future was terrifying. I tried to make as few changes as possible, clinging to a way of life that couldn't last.

There were lighter moments, moments we still laugh about in family reminiscing.

Cary and her friend, Molly, both ten years old, decided to learn to cook. Lindsay and Bruce won the honor of being their guinea pigs. They served as testers of the girls' results. The girls loved to shoo me out of the kitchen and take over. It was fine with me as I busied myself with Lindsay and Bruce. The girls' specialties were to be surprises. The three of us were kept from interfering until the table was set attractively with plates, glasses, napkins and silverware, even flowers from the garden. Each prepared exhibit from the stove was an occasion. That is exactly what happened the day Lindsay and Bruce were called to the kitchen table for a special lunch. They were served a bowl of hot soup.

It appeared to be a fine affair until I noticed a strange green tinge to their soup and a few pieces of something green floating in the bowls. My usual role in their cooking drama was to exclaim over the girls' prowess as budding chefs. That day, I managed to keep Lindsay and Bruce from filling their spoons, while acting my part as doting mother.

"Why don't you tell me what it is before they taste it?" I was more than a little bit concerned. Molly giggled first. Cary tried to keep a straight face. Neither spoke.

"All right," I said. "Come clean. What's in it?" More giggles.

"We made Grass Soup!" I don't know which one said it. I know that they weren't at all chagrined. "We cut grass from the lawn. We boiled it. We put in salt and pepper and some of your somethings from one of those little bottles."

"You mean that you were going to have Lindsay and Bruce eating grass? "It wasn't grass," Cary was not at all apologetic. "It was Grass Soup."

More giggles. It's a story that remains in family lore.

Somehow, my children and I "made it" through those difficult days. They resulted in our becoming a stronger team, moving on and looking forward to the future. Sadly, my husband continued his downhill life. He never resolved his problems and never recovered.

"I'm One of the Girls"

The humiliation and abuse Lindsay suffered in kindergarten made obvious her need of education in a sheltered environment. I was too close to my daughter and too sympathetic to fill the role of teacher. Rather than insist that Lindsay learn the difficult tasks, I did them for her. One solution might be a specially trained teacher to tutor my child. How could such a teacher be found? In the fifties colleges and universities didn't offer training for teachers of children with special needs. And, if some schools did offer such courses, I didn't know how to find them.

After an unproductive search, Lindsay's doctor offered us a surprising opportunity. Lindsay could attend St. Coletta School for Exceptional Children, the acclaimed boarding school in Jefferson, Wisconsin. It was founded by the Sisters of St. Francis especially for children with disabilities. The school's residents included former President John F. Kennedy's sister, Rosemary.

The doctor worried that if I didn't decide immediately, the school's rare vacancy would be taken by another child. I'd been told the gap between my daughter's intellectual growth and that of the typical child would widen each year. Already at eight, when most children are reading and learning arithmetic, Lindsay was learning to dress herself. Lindsay needed what I was unable to provide at home.

Still, I couldn't decide whether St. Coletta's was the best option. The school was hours away. Would Lindsay be frightened so far away? Would strangers understand her limitations? Her trusting innocence tugged at my heart. Would the benefits of the school outweigh her loss of my protection? I procrastinated calling the doctor because of my indecision.

◆•┆◆•┆•◆•

It was one of those sunny Saturdays in January. After several days of heavy snow, drifts were piled five feet high. Busy plows scooped up snow and stacked the powder at curbs, making drifts even higher. The combination of snow-white mountains to climb and soft snow to sculpt provided an invitation children couldn't resist. Cary's friend Molly rang our doorbell.

When I opened the back door, Molly stood there with two more of the girls' playmates, Jean and Betsy. Bundled in shiny nylon snowsuits with fur lined parkas framing faces rosy from the cold, the three looked like miniature Eskimos. Their jackets were dotted with un-melted clumps of white.

"Can Cary come out and play?" Molly asked.

"Come in and get warm." The girls clomped through the door with their boots on. "I'll get Cary," I said. Snow boots, jumbled together, were tossed casually on a rag rug doormat that caught melting drips from the girls' boots as they came into the kitchen. Heat from the oven made the kitchen toasty and filled it with the aroma of baking chocolate chip cookies. Jean pulled down her parka and shook her long brown hair. Molly took off her mittens gingerly, so the snow wouldn't melt up her sleeves. Betsy quickly unzipped her jacket.

When Cary heard her friends' voices, she came running from where she'd been playing with Lindsay. "I'll be ready in a sec," she said, turning to dash toward her bedroom for warm clothing.

"How about some cookies and hot chocolate while you wait?" I asked. An eager chorus of three piped up, "Yes please." If time were not measured in minutes, but rather in how long it took three girls to devour cookies and drink hot chocolate, that's how

"Will I Be on Television?"

long it took for Cary to change clothes and don snow suit, parka and boots. Lindsay, still in her indoor play suit with knitted mukluks on her feet, followed Cary, eagerly tagging along to be part of the fun.

As soon as Cary returned they all clambered into their gear and Betsy pulled open the back door. The four girls spilled out into the snow. "Wait! Where are you going? When will you be back?" I called after them.

"We're staying in your yard," Molly, the last out, turned back with excitement in her voice. "We're making snow angels." They disappeared behind one of the higher drifts and popped up again, laughing on the other side.

As the girls left, I saw the longing in Lindsay's eyes. She looked at me as if to ask, "Why not me?" She didn't want to be left behind. As often happened, I was torn. Lindsay's plight saddened me. Cary was considerate and would have taken Lindsay with her, had I asked. Yet, I feared that, over time, Lindsay could become a burden to her sister. I never pushed including her. Smaller and younger than Cary's friends, Lindsay had difficulty keeping up. Since she had no little friends of her own, Cary's friends became hers, sometimes including her in their fun. Always eager to join them, Lindsay didn't realize her slowness. Undaunted, she wanted to be "one of the girls" and she'd try everything the other youngsters did.

While I pondered, the back door flew open. Cary's head popped in. "Lindsay can come, too." Lindsay lost her forlorn look. A grin filled her entire face. "C'mon, sweetie," let's get you dressed." I led her by the hand to her closet.

Within minutes, zipped into a puffy snow suit, with mittens safely pinned to the cuffs so they wouldn't get lost, Lindsay looked like a tiny space man. *Why must she travel so far away for school?* My indecision crept into that loving moment.

She peered out the window and saw Cary's friends admiring a silly looking snowman they'd just built. She scampered outside to be with them. Then, all the children began making snow angels, lying on their backs and moving their arms and legs in arcs to form wings in the snow. She watched for a few minutes then flopped down on the snow next to Cary. She tried to do exactly what her sister was doing, but couldn't make her arms or legs work in the same way. Puzzled, she stopped in the middle of an arc. She sat bolt upright.

Cary saw her predicament and knelt beside her. She helped Lindsay lie down once again and she moved Lindsay's arms first, then her legs, in the correct pattern. With both hands she pulled her sister to her feet and showed her the angel she'd made.

"Look what Lindsay made," Cary called to the others. Lindsay clapped her mittens together in delight and flopped back down again to make another angel. This time by herself. It became clear that even though she was handicapped, she could learn.

Lindsay's doctor continued to urge me to consider St.Coletta's. One good reason was its excellent reputation. There were others reasons, as well. Both a written description and a photograph of the campus were impressive. Still, my information about the place was limited to phone calls, hearsay and the picture. I worried, too, that Lindsay might not understand her separation from us.

My daughter could grasp only the immediate present. She would have no conception of what she'd face without our support. How could I expect my special child to make such a drastic change?

Summer arrived, longer and hotter than usual. Central air conditioning was uncommon, so on hot afternoons the children cooled themselves by running through the sprinkler. In her yellow tank suit, Lindsay loved dancing through the shower of water. Stopping for a minute to catch her breath, she'd run back the other way as fast as she could. If she stopped for too long, her

"Will I Be on Television?"

brother Bruce would come from behind and chase her through the water again. Indignant, she'd look to me.

"Boosh is chasing me," she'd complain. Then back she'd run through the water. She laughed, danced in circles, and slow trotted after Snowflake, our sable and white collie. She was just as tall as the dog's white mane and liked hanging onto it for balance as she ran. She giggled when Snowflake shook water all over her and was enchanted playing with our collie's six new puppies that closely resembled tan and white teddy bears. I watched, charmed, and wondered what life would be without my beguiling daughter.

That night I tossed about in bed. I got out of bed and paced. Don's lack of interest in the children and his ultimate departure had left me with sole responsibility for their futures. I searched my desk for a pen and tablet. True to my usual practice, I planned to list the pros and cons. Should I send my daughter to St. Coletta's, or should I keep her at home? For over a half-hour I sat at the desk without writing anything. I continued to think of Lindsay's happy times with the family, making snow angels, running through the sprinkler, playing with the puppies, laughing and loving the fun.

She'll never have times like these at school, I thought. Would brief visits home be frequent enough to prevent her loneliness? Who would understand Lindsay's special needs if her family wasn't there to describe them? Who would accept her limitations and not reject her? Was I betraying the confidence of an innocent child who trusted me completely? After a while, it seemed unnecessary to put anything on paper. With my concerns mounting I made a decision not to send Lindsay away.

The next morning I hadn't changed my mind, but when I started dressing my daughter I began to see things differently. At eight years, she couldn't manage the buttons on her blouse. She was able to put on her shoes but she couldn't tie them. Even when I showed her, as I did each day, she couldn't do it by herself. I wasn't trained to teach her how.

Still, it was hard for me to separate St. Coletta's from the institutions the doctors talked about, or from the common phrase, "put her away." Was I putting her away? Was my thinking colored by my own anxiety about what other people would think? Or was I concerned about what the school would be like? My emotions were fighting common sense. I'd been assured that St. Coletta's was a fine place. I couldn't think clearly.

I understood that Lindsay's life would be so much easier with children of similar ability. To become self-sufficient she must learn from someone specially trained to teach her. Years later, there would be professionals in the field who would work with special children, teaching everything from personal essentials to living with others. It was 1961. I'd searched and found no one.

If Lindsay stayed home, Cary and Bruce would eventually outgrow her. She'd have no companions. I'd also heard about young people being embarrassed by a developmentally impaired sibling in their home. Would friends come to visit my other two children, or would they be uncomfortable? Would Cary and Bruce unwittingly push their sister aside?

Do other parents of impaired children go through this agonizing indecision? Lindsay's doctor lost patience with me. "If you don't act quickly the only opening at St. Coletta's will be gone. You have no idea how scarce they are." Pressured, I finally sent the necessary documents to the school, secretly hoping that news of her acceptance would be postponed.

After what seemed like much too short a time, an envelope delivered to our mailbox bore the crest of St. Coletta's. Not eager to read the letter inside, I put the envelope at the bottom of my stacked mail. Long after the children were in bed that night, I opened it. It read, *Your daughter, Lindsay, is accepted for the Fall semester.* Not only did the letter contain a message I didn't want, the date for the beginning of the Fall semester was only two weeks away.

When I sent the application to St. Coletta's, I'd called the school. I was apprehensive about Lindsay's leaving home and the letter answered one of my questions with comforting news. At first, Lindsay wouldn't live in a dormitory. She'd live with a family. Many families moved to Jefferson so their child could attend this excellent school. Lindsay would live with one of them until boarding space at school was available. She'd attend as a day student. For her easier transition it was a good answer. The letter praised a couple named Bartlett. Their daughter, Vicky, was a day student. She'd be Lindsay's companion and "show her the ropes."

The next morning Lindsay and I went to our basement storeroom to choose a suitcase for her trip. She pattered along beside me. She had no idea she'd be leaving her family. I was sure I was betraying her innocent trust. It was hard to tell her. "You'll be going to a wonderful new school," I said with a cheerfulness I didn't feel. I hoped she'd begin to understand and adjust gradually to our being separated. But her thoughts were elsewhere, focused on the moment at hand. "Let's find just the right suitcase." She looked up at me waiting to see what I'd do next. "How do you like this pretty blue one?" I asked, pulling a case out of the storeroom that was the right size. "Bwoo." She lisped, pointing to another suitcase and waiting for me to tell her the color.

"Brown."

"No, bwoo." She liked the first one. She seemed to understand that the suitcase was for her. With pride of possession, she tried to pick it up and drag it toward the stairs. She found it too heavy and looked to me for help. As I carried the suitcase, she climbed the stairs beside me with her tiny hand alongside mine holding tight to the handle and not letting go.

Cary soon joined in the preparations, relishing the part of little mother and teacher. She drew a picture of a small schoolhouse with a bell in the tower and told her sister what she'd learned from me about the school. Cary's picture of the schoolhouse shared the bed that night with Lindsay and a favorite teddy bear. Both went into her suitcase. Bruce was ever present during this family affair, a nuisance with constant questions, "Where is Lindsay going? Why is she going away? How long? Can I go on the train, too?"

Though Lindsay reveled in our attention, it became more difficult for me as the day she'd leave came near. I almost succumbed again, but this time I tried to put my anxiety aside. Having made the decision, I determined to see it through.

"City of Angels"

The Sunday Lindsay and I traveled to Wisconsin was a perfect Indian summer day. Waiting on the platform, watching for the train to St.Coletta's to arrive, Lindsay looked like an angel. She wore a starched white dress with a pink collar, a light weight coat and wrist-length white gloves. She clutched her miniature pink purse in one small hand and I held the other little one in mine.

As this tiny girl, small for her eight years, stared with fascination at the immensity of the locomotive she caught other passengers' smiling attention.

When we were about to board, she gripped my hand tightly. She looked up at me for reassurance. She then planted her feet with stubborn firmness at the bottom of the high iron steps to our carriage car. To her, climbing those steps must have looked like climbing Mount Everest.

A tall uniformed conductor stood at the bottom. He looked down at Lindsay for one moment. "Hello, little lady," he said. "Don't you look pretty?" Without moving from where he stood, he gently scooped her up and deposited her on the platform at the top. She clung to him, hugging his neck, smiling as he set her on her feet. Giving her a soft pat on the top of her head, he turned and offered me his white gloved hand up the steps. With a bow, he doffed his cap.

Soon we were settled in our plush seats. After one testing jerk, the train began to roll. Fascinated, Lindsay tipped her ear toward the clackety-clack of the wheels as the train picked up speed.

As we skimmed across the bright countryside, I pointed out cows, horses and farms, making up stories about them to keep Lindsay entertained and my sadness buried. Crops were lush. Red barns looked like the pictures in children's story books. Some out-buildings had shiny green and yellow tractors parked in front.

Taking in all the sights and sounds, Lindsay stood in her seat and pressed her nose against the train window. When we arrived at the depot in Wisconsin, she skipped along the platform, eager for her next adventure.

Jefferson, called "The City of Angels," was a typical small town. It took only ten minutes for our taxi to deliver us to a verdant campus circled by handsome stone buildings; the entire scene gave the appearance of a well-manicured small college. Approaching the grounds, we saw clusters of children and adults at the door of a chapel. The driver let us off at the stone steps and heavy wooden doorway of what appeared to be the administration building. I lifted Lindsay to ring the doorbell, a treat she always enjoyed. A smiling Sister of St. Francis, in a flowing habit and head-dress, opened the door to a cavernous hall with shining wood floors and a very high heavily-beamed ceiling. Another nun joined her. Lindsay stared up in puzzlement at their black habits. She hung back in bewilderment.

Her small hand in mine turned into a vise-like grip. Then Sister Mary Clare slowly knelt down to my child's height. With a serene, almost beatific, smile on her face and tender, patient movements, she reached out both hands to my daughter. Lindsay let go of my hand and took hers.

For the next hour and a half, I watched my daughter respond enthusiastically in the aura of kindness and understanding from the Sisters who would be caring for her. Seeing her accept them, as she always welcomed new friends, calmed some of my fears. Without realizing, I'd conjured possible hobgoblins in my imagination about the school and its staff. The comfortable reassurance of the Sisters' welcome taught me how wrong I'd been.

We were shown to an empty classroom of small desks where Lindsay would learn. The desks were widely spaced, not crowded together as in some public schools. Children's simple paintings adorned the bulletin board. Because it was Sunday, a chalk drawing of a church decorated the blackboard.

In another room of the dormitory, we saw two walls lined with drawers for students' clothing, neat closets and tidy, sparklingly clean beds. Everywhere the wood floors' pristine shine and the immaculate cleanliness of the buildings impressed me. If the school is this well-maintained, I thought, the children must be given an even greater degree of attention and care.

After our tour of the school, another taxi took us to the Bartlett's. Lindsay would live with the Bartlett family until there was an available bed for her in the school's dormitory. Their house was a single story brick bungalow situated on a quiet street. I saw a neatly kept lawn. Lindsay held my hand as we climbed a few steps to the porch and to the door. With my encouragement she stretched to reach the doorbell. She loved ringing doorbells without my help.

Three Bartletts greeted us. Howard a tall man with a friendly expression looked younger than his gray hair suggested. Jane, in a cool starched Sunday dress with a lace collar, reached out her hand to Lindsay. Vicky, bearing a bland expression, waited quietly behind her parents. Seemingly shy and about twelve-years-old, Vicky fingered a necklace of beads, appearing anxious. Though she attempted a smile, she was obviously ill-at-ease in this social setting. As her parents drew us into their home she followed, more comfortable with Lindsay than with me. I was an adult she didn't know. Her little brother, Jimmie, waiting just inside the door, reminded me of Bruce. Just as Bruce would react, he was eager to be included in the activity.

Howard said, "You ladies will enjoy getting to know each other. My Sunday yard work is calling." He disappeared with Jimmie in tow while Jane and I seated ourselves comfortably in a living room of chintz-upholstered furniture. Freshly cut garden flowers adorned a coffee table and filled the room with fragrance. Suitcase in hand, Vicky led Lindsay toward a hallway that led to the bedrooms. We didn't see the girls again for quite some time.

"Please tell me about Lindsay," Jane said, seating us near a tray on the table. It held two teacups and was filled with pastries. As Jane poured our tea and passed me the pastries, she asked, "What does Lindsay like to do best? What are her favorite foods?" Her next questions were equally down to earth. Clearly, her interest was in making Lindsay feel at home. It didn't take me long to relax, feeling as comfortable with Jane as I would have been with a long-time friend.

After seeing the bedroom where Lindsay would sleep, in a twin bed side-by-side with Vicky's, we unpacked her suitcase. She would have both a five-drawer dresser and a closet of her own. Her accommodations in the Bartlett home were more than generous. In those short hours in Jefferson I put aside many of my concerns. I was caught up in the mid-western warmth of small town Wisconsin.

Too soon, it was time to leave the Bartlett's pleasant surroundings. For a few minutes I stood in the kitchen doorway and watched Lindsay, sitting at a table listening intently to Vicky. During pauses in the conversation, the girls were happily sipping chocolate milk. It did my heart good to see how well she was responding to Vicky. For the longest time, she didn't realize I was standing there.

"Sweetheart," I said to my daughter who put aside her milk when she finally saw me. "I have to say goodbye now." Lindsay made a move to get up from her chair. I stopped her. She was having such a pleasant time, I didn't want to interrupt.

"Will I Be on Television?"

In those few moments what became apparent was something I'd never before considered. Lindsay was extremely comfortable with someone more like herself. She must have sensed an affinity for Vicky and a soothing familiarity. Vicky lived with similar challenges. For the first time ever, I put myself in Lindsay's place. How difficult it must it be for her and these special children to live in our world. In our world, they are constantly forced to reach for unreachable goals. The daily courage and accompanying frustration they live with is unimaginable. Lindsay never complains, but what must it be like for her? My gratitude for the world of St. Coletta's school grew. I realized for the first time that for Lindsay to be among children who had needs similar to her own could be a blessing.

"Would you like to stay here with Vicky?" I asked her. She nodded her head and sat down again. "How would you like to sleep here? Remember, we unpacked your suitcase?" Lindsay nodded again. I suspected she was thinking of this as another adventure in a day filled with them. She seemed completely at ease.

"I may not see you for a while." I cleared my throat to keep my voice calm.

"Remember the school we visited? That's your new school. You'll go there with Vicky, and you'll live here with Vicky and her mother and daddy and Jimmie. I know you're going to like it." Lindsay smiled at Vicky. I hoped she understood that I wouldn't be nearby. "I'll call you every day," I said. There seemed nothing more to say. My eyes filled with silent tears. They were more for me and the loneliness I would feel than for my daughter.

—◆·❙·◆·❙·◆·—

It's called "separation anxiety," particularly difficult for parents of children with special needs, who are more dependent than other children. But my anxiety wasn't permitted to last long, thanks to a taxi driver with a vocal zeal for his home town. "Name's Benjamin," he said, driving me back to the railroad station. "Call me Ben." In farm jeans, shirt sleeves rolled up, and with a fly-fishing bait pinned to his baseball cap, he might well have been chairman of the local Chamber of Commerce. The real chairman could have done no better job regaling a visitor with the many offerings of the city of Jefferson. "Sort of a German city with historic buildings and warm-hearted folks," Ben told me.

"Do ya like to fish? "Did ya know we're on two rivers?" he asked, not waiting for an answer. "Ya like white bass? Ya should see the big walleyes. If I could take my hands off this here steering wheel I'd show ya how big." His familiarizing of the word "you" sounded much like many boys with whom I'd grown up. I became as comfortable in Jefferson as Lindsay had appeared to be.

Laughing out loud, he told me fish stories. He had me laughing with him. By the time we arrived at the train station he'd learned that I, too, loved to fish. "Ben," I told him, "I was the only child of a sportsman father who wanted a boy. So, he taught me everything he would have taught a boy." That sentence pleased Ben. The drive flew by on the heels of his fascinating conversation, activated more heartily by his receiving that bit of information from me.

At the station, as Ben helped carried my suitcase and settled me in the waiting room, he said. "Don't worry. Your little girl'll be o.k," He patted my arm. "The Bartletts are fine folks." Over his shoulder as he walked back toward the taxi stand, he called, "See ya soon, I hope." It wasn't long before the early evening train arrived to take me back to Minneapolis. On this run it wasn't nearly as full as it had been on our earlier journey.

After a relaxing supper in the dining car I found my seat in the almost empty coach once again. It seemed unusual not to have Lindsay at my side awaiting my help. Alone, I watched out the window into blackness as the train moved through the dark night toward home.

Astonishingly, I was startled by a very real physical sensation. It felt like an extremely heavy weight lifted from my shoulders. It was a feeling of lightness and relief. Until that moment, I'd never felt that Lindsay's care and welfare was a heavy weight or a burden. If it was, I carried it willingly. Nor did I consider the responsibility heavier because I carried it alone.

The unexpected physical reaction must have been the result of my knowing that I'd resolved the long-term troubling questions of Lindsay's future at last. Looking back through the telescope of sixty-years, I realize that the important decision to send my daughter to St. Coletta's School was one of the hardest decisions I ever made and one of the very best.

"Whatever Puts a Sparkle in a Child's Eyes"

Lindsay's reaction to being separated from our family wasn't at all what I'd expected. She banished all my imagined worries with a single abrupt answer. On my next visit to her at school, I asked, "Were you scared the day I took you to your new school and I went home?" She didn't hesitate a second before answering, "No." Her quizzical expression read, "Why would you ask?" For Lindsay, it was the beginning of a new adventure. My conjecture about her being at ease with children having needs similar to hers' was correct. As we slowly walked around the school campus and Lindsay met a few of her friends, it became obvious that she'd blended well into her new situation.

I was the one suffering from loneliness. Though busy with Cary and Bruce, I badly missed my little girl. I would find myself looking over my shoulder for the tiny sprite that rarely left my side and feel a clutching emptiness when she wasn't there. During her first two weeks away I called her every evening. Jane, who took my calls, was generous with detailed reports. Then Lindsay was handed the phone. Answering my questions about how she was doing, she'd say, "Fine," or "Good," with her familiar one-word replies. Despite her short answers, her pleasure with her new friend Vicky came through the telephone wires. It was obvious in the tone of her voice when I mentioned Vicky's name.

After being continually reassured by her happiness when we talked, I had an increased sense of comfort. It was not as profound as the feeling of relief that came over me on my train ride home from Jefferson nor as emotional. Rather, it was common sense that made me realize Lindsay was being better-cared-for at St. Coletta's and the Bartletts than I could care for her at home. She would learn more than I could ever teach her. She would gain an ability to become more independent. I willingly spaced my calls farther apart. I felt at ease waiting for another visit until she'd been away for six weeks. An appointment for a meeting with Mother Superior was standard after a new student had been attending the school for six weeks.

Late October in Wisconsin can be the climax of breathtaking bursts of orange and the yellows and reds of Fall maples or it could be a cold, rainy, dismal introduction to Winter. There seems to be no in-between. Upon my arrival in Jefferson for the Fall visit there was no mistaking that I'd been lucky. I could barely keep my eyes on the road while admiring the town's sunlit green lawns, strikingly accented by vibrant colors everywhere I looked. In cars, sightseers crept along slowly, holding up traffic.

St. Coletta's administration building, atop its grassy knoll overlooking the town's main throughway, was even more handsome than I remembered. To reach it I drove on narrow streets through Jefferson. This typical 1940's small Midwest town with its frame houses, shutters, porches, picket fences and well-tended gardens had a charm of its own. At a filling station an obviously handicapped young man, perhaps a graduate of St. Coletta's, filled my car's gas tank.

The administration building's stone and brick blended perfectly into surrounding gardens. Other buildings, spaced short distances away, were similar in their architecture. This visit provided time for me to look more closely at the campus. The vista and gardens were like a beautiful watercolor of nature. As I

"Will I Be on Television?"

drove up the hill to the main building I felt enveloped by an aura of peacefulness.

Mother Superior awaited me in her office. Clothed in her nun's habit, black from head to foot, wearing a wimple that covered her hair, she stood tall and erect. She was immediately intimidating. In contrast to her awe-inspiring presence, the white of her headpiece framed the most serene face I'd ever encountered.

"It's a pleasure to meet you," she said. The warmth of her voice was a welcoming contrast to the formality of her appearance. "I'm happy to report that Lindsay is adjusting quite well," she continued.

We were standing a few steps into her office. Moving toward her desk, she motioned me to the chair in front of it. As she seated herself behind the desk, she said, "I'm sorry we didn't have room for your daughter as a boarding student immediately, but she seems happy with the Bartletts." She smiled, "We've known them for a long time and they are a fine family. They will take good care of her. Lindsay and Vicky have already become good friends."

Her good news came as no surprise. Lindsay was a cooperative unquestioning child. She was comfortable with decisions made for her. My concern had been that she'd be lonely away from her family. Succeeding on-her-own was a courageous accomplishment.

"We can tell Lindsay's had loving care." Mother Superior said. The more she talked, the less intimidating she seemed. "I'd like to know more about your daughter," she said. "We know only what was on the application and that is always too brief."

She was an attentive listener as I recounted Lindsay's history. At times, she stopped me to ask a question or make a comment about my daughter's rate of development or her physical and psychological workups. About Lindsay's diagnosis she said, "I'm familiar with the catch-all phrase, mentally retarded."

In those days, specific diagnoses weren't freely offered to parents. Doctors were familiar with mental retardation but most were general practitioners, not specialists. My experience was that they were close-mouthed when it came to children that did not fit the norm. After a while I'd stopped seeking a more specific diagnosis. My questions were evaded if I attempted to probe. The emphasis was not on what could help Lindsay, instead it was on predicting her desolate future and attempting to convince me that our family would be better off without her.

It wasn't until Lindsay was in her fifties that a pediatric specialist told me her symptoms of heavy weight and unresponsiveness, the morning after her crisis, were caused by "oxygen deprivation." Unspoken was, "resulting in brain damage." His spur-of-the-moment diagnosis was more accurate than anything I'd learned previously. Seeing my surprise at hearing what I'd always conjectured but had never been told, he immediately changed the subject and would say no more. I never understood why.

After hearing Lindsay's history, Mother Superior spoke of her future at St. Coletta's. Describing the school's approach to special education, she said, "First, the children are taught to care for their personal needs. It's obvious that Lindsay learned quite a bit at home, but there are new skills needed for her to be at the level of self-sufficiency suitable to her capability. Lindsay will be taught academic subjects geared to her intellectual age; reading, writing and arithmetic. She'll progress at her own rate, in ways to help her adapt to as well-rounded a life as possible." She added, "I hope there will be an available boarding vacancy next year."

After speaking of St. Coletta's values, "Creating a caring community and sharing compassion for others," she offered me a tour of the school and a visit to Lindsay's classes. She called one of the other Sisters to show me around. By the time I left her, Mother Superior no longer intimidated me. Rather, her gentleness and insight into what the children in her care needed gave me infinite confidence in my daughter's future.

Sister Mary Clare, soft-spoken and thoughtful, led me on a tour that began with an immaculate dormitory room with walls of drawers to hold the children's clothing, and wood floors so highly polished they almost mirrored our steps. I was then given fifteen minutes in the school's chapel. Framed by a vaulted ceiling, candles glimmered at the beautiful altar while I knelt wrapped in the warmth of peaceful solitude.

After that, we visited Lindsay's classroom. My daughter was one of seven children of varying ages. One boy appeared to be about twelve. Three boys and girls were perhaps five or six. The others' ages were mixed. Each sat at a small table set with utensils, placemats and napkins, in a space of their own. The youngsters were being taught how to eat and behave at meals. Extremely patient, the Sister teaching the class worked with each student individually, giving lessons as basic as using a knife and fork correctly. The exercises became instilled. Lindsay still asks, "How are my table manners?"

When my child saw me walk in the door, she looked at the Sister teaching the class, as if asking permission to come to me. She received a nod and came to where I stood, with a smile that lighted her entire face. I couldn't help tearing up when I leaned down to give her a hug.

After a few minutes, she dutifully returned to her table and I was led to the far side of the room to observe the class. Watching Lindsay was particularly interesting. Each time the students were given an instruction and expected to follow it she looked to me, seeking help before attempting the task. The reaction must have been instilled when I did the tasks for her, rather than teaching her to accomplish them herself. That brief observation made clear why children learn more readily without parents present.

Howard, a boy of about ten, looking like a Norman Rockwell drawing with red hair and freckles, was seated a distance from the others. He was a handsome boy who looked the least impaired of the group. He'd watched me from the time I entered the room. I couldn't help looking his way. But when I did, he abruptly put his head down on his table with his hands over his ears. He wouldn't look up. After a while of being left alone, he raised his head, but always with his hands over his ears. If I inadvertently glanced in his direction, his head would go down again. The teacher explained that he feared unexpected noise and being close to the other children. In the future, his behavior would be diagnosed as autism. In those years the word 'autism' didn't exist.

Symptoms of another child I saw that day would eventually be diagnosed as either autism or Aspberger's syndrome. Mannerisms of this tiny girl were different from what most consider the norm. It wasn't easy to point to the subtle differences in her appearance, but they were present.

About seven years old, she had a bland baby face and curly golden hair. When we were nearby, I said to her, "My name's Jan, what's your name?" attempting to be friendly. Rapidly and seemingly angry, she sat down in the middle of the floor, refusing to get up. She wouldn't cooperate when asked to stand. After giving the child time to calm down, her teacher walked patiently toward the door with two other youngsters. Perceiving she was left behind, the girl, Judy, reluctantly stood up and followed them. Watching, I made a mental note to learn more about the cause of this unusual behavior and how teachers worked with these children.

Times and attitudes began to change in the 70s. During those years, and from that time on, I began hearing about autism. I discovered that psychiatric specialists, anthropologists and researchers were providing important information about the autism spectrum. Howard and Judy's conditions would be included in descriptions of "autism spectrum disorders." The autism syndrome, itself, as eventually defined, was "the abnormal development of social relationships and the obsessive desire for the maintenance of sameness." An autistic child might not be able to bear looking directly at unfamiliar people. Another might be aggressive or scream at change. One youngster could be unusually

"Will I Be on Television?"

repetitive in speech. Another's parents might be embarrassed by their child's appearance and behavior and want the child removed from their home.

The teachers at St. Coletta's knew that early teaching of speech and social interaction is important. While some children remain socially too awkward to be independent, others become adults who are able to be successful in diverse ways.

My instruction in how children with special needs were taught began with the single sentence of a friend who was one of the earliest trained teachers of special needs children. She taught classes in public schools for years and is the author of a training manual. She said, "We learn through different senses, by hearing, by seeing, by touching or by movement — sometimes by one of those, sometimes by a combination." Her words piqued my curiosity about the ways she translated senses into instruction.

Rosemary taught several ages of youngsters in one class at the same time. She described her methods. She spoke of examples of touch, to teach a child to spell his name. "We cut letters from sandpaper, let him feel and re-arrange them. We have them draw their name in chocolate pudding, or with Play-Doh, or they shape it with rope.

"Bringing animals into the classroom teaches socialization, how to touch other people gently and care for them," she said. "The children loved the hamsters and bunnies that I brought to class.

"Instead of reading a book to learn arithmetic, we made cakes using measuring cups. M&M's, Cheerios and raisins teach fractions."

"How do you discover what works for each child?" I asked.

"Trial and error," she smiled. "Whatever puts the sparkle in a child's eyes." She described pinning large sheets of white paper on the class walls and giving the children magic markers to write or draw as they pleased. "The children would ask for the *wallpaper* to be pinned up."

She talked of trips to a skating rink — where some loved walking on the ice when they weren't able to skate — of a ride on a plane, of using puzzles and Legos.

"Whatever is different," she said. "We changed activities often, tried many new things. We set up play stations for smaller groups, with short turns at each station."

Her class included children with IQs from 40 to 80. "At the time, mine was the only class. They threw everyone in," she laughed. This exceptional educator, along with three others, wrote the text book used to train teachers in the county.

Long before there were Special Education classes in public schools, the Sisters of St. Coletta's must have known what I later learned, for they built a lasting foundation for Lindsay's success, despite her limitations.

"Of Course I'm an Angel"

Lindsay surprised us. At St. Coletta's, in no time at at all, she learned how to dress herself, to bathe, to comb her hair, button her buttons and tie her shoes, all without someone standing by to help. A few touches to her hair, or her dress straightened a bit, was all the help she needed. Her accomplishment gave her a new self-confidence.

During the night of her first long weekend at home, I slipped into the shadows of her room as she slept. As I stood watching for the longest time, an overwhelming wave of tenderness touched me. She slept peacefully. She wore a half-smile. My doubts about sending her away at such a young age began to ease.

Her academic classes began with instruction in elementary reading and writing. While Lindsay found reading to be a formidable stumbling block, writing came more easily. One afternoon, Bruce excitedly raced to the house from our roadside mailbox, waving a note and shouting, "Mom, Lindsay can write."

Large irregular letters, *d ea rmo the r*, not in a straight line but in a circle, were inscribed in heavy pencil on the page flapping in his hand. Though Lindsay's lettering was far from perfect, the unexpected note made my heart leap. I pictured her determination, pouring over that sheet of paper and forming each letter with great pains. The reverse side of the paper held a brief note from Sister Mary Clare, "It's a joy to share Lindsay's accomplishment." The Sister deserved credit for countless hours spent unearthing the buried treasure of my daughter's ability. It was this individual attention that guided Lindsay through the pitfalls of growing up, of mastering what she would otherwise never have attempted.

Around the same time there was an article in the newspaper about a distraught mother who found her son in a deplorable condition, warehoused in a public facility for the mentally impaired. She described another boy banging himself against a wall. Later, that facility was closed. In 1959 the Minnesota legislature studied the "Needs of Institutions," but it wasn't until the 1960s that Congress in Washington took notice. The first step toward education of the handicapped was earmarking small amounts of federal funds for special education classes. Improvements followed, but slowly. Even decades later, unmet needs remained. In the early fifties there were few schools like St. Coletta's. Lindsay was one of the fortunate.

Despite living away, Lindsay kept her important place in our hearts. Long before her visits, Cary and Bruce began planning. Though Lindsay never asked for anything, they'd march through the house chanting in rhythm, "What Lindsay wants, Lindsay gets. What Lindsay wants, Lindsay gets." It was their favorite ploy, for they turned her times at home into the special treats they liked best; the picnics, the Zoo, the State Fair, feeding the ducks at their grandfather's favorite pond. Lindsay went along happily. Her visits home became the best of times, fun for the whole family. Through the years we often retold stories of Lindsay's antics.

As the children grew, Cary and Bruce remained entirely unconcerned about her disability. That she was always included in family activities provided much of the foundation for her later social skills. Being the middle child, sandwiched between two exuberant beings close to her age, she had no choice but to join in, and her siblings didn't cater to her special needs.

"Will I Be on Television?"

She trotted after the two of them, never questioning when they urged her to play the role of 'straight man' in their comedy threesome. They re-named themselves, The Three Stooges, Curly, Larry and Moe. Cary was Moe, Bruce was Curly and Lindsay was Larry, because she was the chubby one. Apparently, so was Larry.

Lindsay's guileless way of cooperating in whatever pranks her sister and brother invented, produced all too frequent jokes, *on me*. During one of her visits they took full advantage of her naivety. While I was distracted by a phone call, the two could hardly wait for me to discover the mischief they'd concocted. Seemingly appalled, with loud voices in unison, they tattled as if they were reporting the newspaper headline of the day, "Mom! Lindsay's gone."

Aghast, I checked the house. Lindsay was nowhere to be seen. I ran outdoors and looked in the yard. Then, I saw the two culprits, with their hands over their mouths, stifling laughter. "All right, where did you hide Lindsay?" I demanded. So much for that! Delighting in their game of hide-and-seek, they wouldn't tell. At least I knew Lindsay wasn't lost or in trouble. I recognized that I was the one being teased. They gave me no choice but to cooperate and become "seeker" in their game. After what seemed too long a search, again throughout the house, Lindsay squeezed herself up from behind a couch, where the two had hidden her. "April Fool!" they giggled. Lindsay chimed in with her lisp, "Apwil Foo." Her grin was a mile wide. In my dismay, I'd completely forgotten it was April first. We celebrated the "found" sister with cookies and milk.

During another vacation, my enthusiastic daughter told a neighbor, Marion, about her school's Christmas pageant. Marion asked, "Are you going to be an angel?"

"Of course!" Lindsay proclaimed, insulted, her hands on her hips, her self-satisfied expression far from angelic. Telling about the conversation later, Marion found it hard to keep from laughing as she talked. She said, "The look on Lindsay's face almost shouted, "How could I dare think that she'd be anything *but* an angel."

Our family changed. Don was no longer interested in the four of us, and with Lindsay far from home there was no need to remain in Minneapolis. Temporarily, we moved nearer my parents' home in Milwaukee and only an hour-and-a-half's drive from St. Coletta's.

Cary adapted quickly and parlayed her generous nature and sense of responsibility into the role of a care-taker; quick to come to the aid of anyone who might need help. When her Home Economics class included a short course on hair styling, she put her skill to work during a visit to Lindsay. Seeing Cary fix a ribbon to her sister's hair, two small girls with the round faces of Down syndrome tugged at her skirt pleading, "Do me! Do me!"

Taking turns holding brightly colored ribbons to their hair, they preened and strutted like fashion models. Soon their hair was brushed to a shine with a ribbon tied in. Almost dancing a jig, they passed a looking glass back and forth. The sparkle in their almond eyes could have lighted the room.

Driving home, enthused by the success of her venture, Cary suggested taking the members of her Girl Scout troop to St. Coletta's to style more children's hair. At first impression the idea seemed excellent.

The children at school would look pretty and have an enjoyable day with the Scouts. But I had misgivings. Cary's young friends were unacquainted with handicapped youngsters. For those unfamiliar with the disabled, a first meeting can be distressing. Actions and reactions of the children could be unexpected. I remembered that I'd not known how to approach disabled people. It was only when I was able to get past being put off by unfamiliar facial features or unaccustomed behavior that

"Will I Be on Television?"

my heart made room for their charm. Also, the children at St. Coletta's might pull away if they sensed any Scout's discomfort.

I mentioned my concerns to both Cary and Mother Superior, but their belief in the project convinced me to proceed. On the chosen day we set off. Two mothers, two cars, six girls. Spic and span in their green Scout uniforms, the girls were anticipating a great adventure. The cars were alive with chatter, laughter, camp songs and arms out the windows to wave to each other when the two cars met at stop lights. The words to the song "Make new friends and keep the old, some are silver and the others gold," became indelibly engraved on my mind as the girls sang it over and over. The words were perfectly appropriate for the day's activity.

Two of the Scouts knew Lindsay and had some idea of what to expect. The four others had never encountered anyone disabled. Despite the fun, my questions resurfaced. *Would the girls be understanding of the children's plight and accept them as they were? Would the school children sense any unconscious discomfort and not welcome their visitors?*

I settled on trying to prepare the Scouts in advance. *But how?* How does one describe differences from the norm in appearance, or some of the unusual behavior I'd encountered during past visits? Should I focus on the children as a group or on individuals? I was flying blind. It seemed best to talk about the children I knew; calling them by name and emphasizing their good qualities rather than their handicaps. Still, it was important to realistically share what the girls should expect upon meeting the other youngsters, lest they be caught unaware.

As we approached St. Coletta's, I hoped that the others could feel the peacefulness that the stately buildings and beauty of the manicured grounds always gave me. All the more this time, for as we drove onto the grounds, one of the questions I struggled with was being answered. On the lawn a nun, the folds of her habit looking like a black kite about to soar, ran with a ball in her arms.

She tossed it to the boy of about ten who was playing with her. He ran as fast as he was able, for quite a distance, until he could retrieve the ball and throw it back. It was immediately apparent that his gait was unusual. He ran stiff-legged, his legs straight as poles. His arms were outstretched sideways as he chased the rolling ball.

Near it, he stared at the ball for some time before picking it up and attempting to throw. When he finally threw the ball, the nun caught it closer to where he stood. Quickly covering the distance between them, she patted his back and gave him a hug. The girls in our car watched the pantomime attentively, not commenting. The tender scene of interaction with someone different from themselves provided the answer for me. It was the perfect example for the girls.

In the parking lot, when the Scouts gathered awaiting directions and eager to go to the children, I said. "Let's talk for a few minutes before we go to the dormitory." They listened with interest as I talked about the boy playing ball. "Did you notice that he didn't run the way boys usually run?" Some of the girls said yes," others nodded. "You'll be working with children who are different.

Cary's sister, Lindsay, is different from what you'd expect. But just as the boy tried hard to play the game, these children try hard to do what's expected of them…or what we hope for them to be able to do."

Mentioning the names of some of the children they'd meet caught their attention. "Some of the little girls have round faces and different shaped eyes," I said. "Or if one of the children doesn't look at you, it doesn't mean she wants you to go away." The girls seemed to understand. The words they responded to most readily were, "The children want to be loved just as the rest of us want to be loved." *That day's events, and similar experiences, when I prepared others to meet Lindsay, taught me the importance of advance preparation.*

"Will I Be on Television?"

It was gratifying to see the way the young children responded to the Scouts' knowing their names and something about them. Two of Cary's friends worked with Betsy and Susan, cousins with symptoms that later would be called Down syndrome. Both children were out-going, hugging their new friends and persisting in teasing them; snatching brushes, combs and ribbons, laughing and messing up their carefully styled hair. The Scouts exhibited exceptional patience, playing the little children's game. Eventually, the two settled down long enough to have their hair styled again. Peering into hand mirrors, they tipped them up and down and sideways, excited to study the final results.

———•ı•ı•———

In the 50s and 60s, though Down syndrome was commonplace, it was hidden at home or in an institution. It was briefly described in psychology books, but identified by a different insensitive name. Those afflicted were called Mongoloids. Slowly, as time passed, attitudes began to change. If those two little girls had been born fifty years later, and lived to be teenagers, they might have gained prized spots on a cheer-leading team or learned to surf. They might have been elected Prom Queen of their high school class, as was a Texas teenager with Down syndrome in 2010. In 2011, they could have a date and attend a Special Needs Prom for young people just like themselves.

The term Asperger's didn't come into widespread use until the 1990s. The word Autism was so unfamiliar that when the father of a child with Asperger's talked about his charitable teaching of other autistic children, the word was frequently misunderstood to mean "artistic."

In the 90s, the number of children diagnosed with autism increased, as did research to determine the cause. Special needs education and available public and private resources increased as well, but slowly. Charitable foundations and support organizations were formed. Parents and individual benefactors took part. Though efforts strengthened, the need continued to grow, perpetually leaving a void remaining to be filled.

―・◆・❙・◆・❙・◆・―

Later that afternoon at St. Coletta's, the Scouts were introduced to autistic children. First it was Isabelle, the blonde curly-haired little girl who'd refused to move from the floor the last time I visited. Jane, the most mature of the Scouts, was standing nearest to the child. She maintained a short distance, but watched Isabelle while seeming to ignore her. Left alone, Isabelle was attracted by the bright ribbons Jane held in her hand. Jane walked slowly toward the child, speaking quietly in warm and friendly tones. Isabelle was now a more cooperative child than when I'd last seen her. It happens over time that autistic children become more used to others, and Jane's manner with the child put Isabelle at ease.

As she came closer, Jane held out a brush that Isabelle looked at with a measure of fear. She wouldn't touch the brush immediately. But after watching the other girls working with children across the room and seeing they were not being hurt when their hair was brushed, Isabelle took the brush from Jane and awkwardly stroked her own curls. This was quite a step for the child. Some autistic youngsters can't stand to have their hair touched. Isabelle was showing her confidence in Jane's patient, restrained approach and gentle voice.

Next, Jane helped her choose a bright red ribbon, but Isabelle wouldn't release her end of the ribbon long enough for Jane to put it in her hair. Instead, she waved it dancing and spinning in the air, looking at it with delight. When Jane eventually managed to pin a red bow in Isabelle's soft brown curls, we two mothers watching the scene, from its slow beginning to its satisfying end, were too moved to speak.

Sister Mary Clare, pleased with Jane's success, took the remaining Scouts in tow and talked to them about the way to approach autistic children. She led them toward two girls in

"Will I Be on Television?"

school pinafores, seated at tables a distance from the others. Sister Mary Clare stayed with the four of them. She hoped that the children would be unafraid because she was standing by.

She instructed the Scouts to sit quietly and let the younger ones touch the brushes and ribbons. She suggested that this time the visitors style each other's hair, showing the autistic children it was a harmless activity. Eventually, one of the children let her hair be brushed, but the other child remained too fearful and sensitive to have anyone touch her. Shortly afterward, the Scouts returned to the larger group of children and the other little ones swooped in for good-bye hugs. It was easy to see how they tugged at the heartstrings of the Scouts, who found it hard to leave and promised to return.

Returning to the cars, we had no idea of the surprise that awaited us. As we drove toward the school's entrance another car approached. Drawing closer, we could identify two of the three people in the vehicle as nuns from the school. One drove. Another in back was seated next to a small passenger. They came from the only house at the farthest end of a winding road that seemed to gently meander through an empty sea of high grass.

When they neared, I recognized that the other person in the back seat was President John F. Kennedy's sister, Rosemary. For many years, Rosemary lived at St. Coletta's, tenderly cared for by the sisters.

That encounter created one more anecdote in the Scouts' oft-retold stories of the day. Each girl earned a treasured memory along with her merit badge. In their talk of the day with each other, it was easy to discern an increased understanding of others' challenges. Cary's memories were added to the family lore of Lindsay's years at school.

An occasion our family, grandparents and friends, celebrated for almost a week, was Lindsay's first Holy Communion. In white organdy with a white veil, she appeared much as the angel she'd pictured herself to Marion. But with imagined halo askew, she kept us laughing with silly antics and few signs of angelic behavior.

More seriously and for quite a while, my daughter began to question my role in her life. Truly puzzled, time and again she'd ask, "Are you my real mother?" Though she'd address her letters to me *Dear Mother,* as she was instructed, I guessed that she might be confused because of the name and persona of Mother Superior at school.

For too long, I didn't give her question the thought it deserved. Each time she'd ask, "Are you my real mother," I'd answer, "of course," believing that answer would suffice. Too late to save her genuine worry, I realized that her puzzlement wasn't going away. Her question deserved more serious attention than it was getting. We had several quiet talks. I explained slowly, many times over, that I was proud to be her mother and would never give up that honor. My continued reassurance satisfied her. She never asked again.

It was also during her St. Coletta's years that Lindsay developed her complete honesty and lack of guile — at times, abrupt honesty! It was a given fact in our family that if ever we wanted the unadulterated answer to a question, with no frills, tact or adjectives to get in the way, we'd ask Lindsay. We just had to be prepared for some surprising answers. For example, one day, years later, Lindsay and I talked about her memories of school.

"What do you remember?" I asked.

"They taught dresser drawers." I wasn't sure what she meant, and asked her. "To dress neatly, she said. "To fold clothes. I wasn't good at that."

"What else?" She pondered for a time, "Clean my room every Saturday, reading, writing, arithmetic, spelling bees and guess what? I came in second! That's all I can remember...I think."

"What did you like best?"

"Will I Be on Television?"

"Nothing !" That answer was typical of Lindsay's being guileless. Among our family members and friends, we know that if we want an absolutely straight, honest answer, we'd better be prepared for one from Lindsay. Like many children, Lindsay couldn't appreciate the privilege and great good of her education. Her memories matched those of a few of our friends who were taught to behave and to learn in a strict Catholic school.

But, of course, my appreciation of St. Coletta's was absolutely the opposite of Lindsay's memory of the strictness of the nuns. I remain too well aware that the sisters rescued my daughter from a life of potential tragedy. They nourished her intellectual capacity to its maximum. They cultivated her emotional intelligence in place of her lack of mental ability. They sowed the seeds of a productive future. Despite an IQ of 62, Lindsay developed into a courageous, likable Miss Personality during those years. Ever since, she's continued to keep those of us who admire her spirit either surprised, or laughing, or both.

What would have become of our Easter baby had the recommendations of the 50's been followed? *I interpreted the doctors' recommendations as put her in one of the frightful public institutions of the time and forget her.*

"I Felt Terrible. I was Scared. I was Petrified."

Ambulance sirens screamed. Red lights flashed. Voices shouted. My legs were shattered. I couldn't move. Blood rushed from my slashed knees onto the smoking engine that pinned me. I was conscious, but shock wiped away the pain.

Hours earlier, without a care in the world, Bruce and I set off in my new Lark station wagon to visit Lindsay at St. Coletta's. The car, a jaunty small machine, burnished black, iridescent in the sun, had cool red leather seats. I was proud to own her and relished every excuse to be on the road.

July 9th, 1962, a bright and crisp day, felt just hot enough for us to keep all the windows open, catching the breeze as we traveled. We laughed as we rode; singing silly songs off key, embarking on an adventure. Sometimes we counted cows in the sun washed fields we passed, or we played 20 questions.

Long before seatbelts were standard equipment, Bruce, at seven, squirmed in his seat, switching positions, looking out the window or leaning over his seat back to fish something to eat from a surprise packet on the seat behind him. Often he'd ask, "How long before we get there?" a question that would prompt a new game that would keep him occupied. In the early 60s Wisconsin country roads were still two lanes and narrow. Beginning with the final third of the way to Jefferson, our narrow road had only a thin line of dusty shoulder on the passenger side of the car. A deep ditch bordered the skimpy shoulder.

As we approached a rise in the roadway, I could see a line of what looked like eight or ten cars coming toward us. They poked slowly along down the slight slope in the other lane of the two-lane country road. A slow-moving bright green farm tractor driven by a farmer perched high on its metal seat blocked the creeping parade. I slowed our car as the line drew near. My plan was to get back to our normal speed after the stream of cars passed. We watched the tractor and its parade approach us.

Without warning, a large sedan flew out from the pack at high speed. It barreled headlong at our car. Fear of getting off the road only to flip over into the ditch clutched me. I couldn't make my hands react. I froze at the wheel. Bruce shouted. *"That car's going to hit us!"* He shattered my trance. I wrenched the steering wheel hard right to escape. The huge sedan exploded into the left front of our car. A blinding, brilliant white light surrounded us. Then, a death-like stillness. Nothing stirred. I heard no sound. Choking, acrid smoke filled the Lark. Hot steam spewed from the cracked engine.

My son lay crumpled under the dashboard. He didn't move or speak. His glassy eyes were blank. His face ran red with blood. The fractured white bone of his smashed leg terrified me. I tried to reach Bruce but I couldn't. The only part of my body that would move was my head. I could barely turn it. My car's front tire pinned my left leg to the driver's seat. The engine pinned my right leg and the rest of me. Breaking the long unearthly silence, I heard men's voices and children crying. I called out, "Please help my son!"

"There's a child in this car." A man heard and shouted to others. They wrestled with the slashed metal of the passenger door. The crumpled steel took the strength of more than one man to pry it open. Thankfully, Bruce was alive, but his eyes didn't focus. His face bore the staring mask of shock as the men lifted

"Will I Be on Television?"

him out. I couldn't see where he was taken. I couldn't see beyond the car door. I could move my eyes, but my head would move only slightly.

Alone in the car, still conscious, I saw blood pooling on my knees. My knees didn't look right. The grimy front tire was almost in my lap. I could have picked stones from between its treads if I'd been able to move my arm. The Lark's engine clamped my right leg. Bone was exposed by a gash that split my knee wide open.

The crackled glass of the windshield framed an open jagged hole. The steering wheel pressed against my chest. It was an effort to breathe. But strangely I felt no pain. I was told it was because I was in shock.

I don't know how long I sat in that position listening to voices at a distance. I only know it seemed like too long a time. I wanted to shout once more, but couldn't. I wanted to tell someone of the urgency of getting me out of the car. The blow from the steering wheel caused blood to flow into my chest. My breathing became more difficult by the moment. The voices came closer and a man stood at my open window. We'll get you out," he said.

"You'll need a hydraulic jack." I managed. That's the last thing I remember until the hydraulic jack and many gentle hands pulled me from the wreckage. I have no memory of how they cut me out of the mangled metal or were able to lift the tire and engine from my legs. I only recall hearing a siren and sensing flashing red lights. When I awakened again, I was lying on a stretcher in what seemed to be a large room. I was fighting with all of my strength to breathe.

Gasping, drowning in the blood in my chest, panicked, pleading with God to be able to catch even one short breath, I prayed. I prayed fervently, as my last chance. Suddenly and immediately, I felt myself in a space of awesome and overwhelming peace. I was wrapped in an aura of golden light. It surrounded me. I was able to breathe easily with no effort. Those few moments, breathing freely once again and clothed in the warmth of astonishing peace, I knew without question that I would get well.

Later in the night, I was transported from the hospital where I lay to another hospital thirty miles away, a hospital specially equipped to care for my severe injuries. Even the medics didn't believe I'd survive the ambulance ride to the second hospital. I was the only one who knew I'd get well. I couldn't tell anyone why I knew. For years, I didn't speak of the profound phenomenon I'd been blessed by in the first hospital. It was too powerful, too sacred, to put into mere words.

Vaguely, I recall the motion of the ambulance. Then nothing, until I awakened in a hospital bed to see my mother and father standing at my bedside. They'd sped from their home to this hospital for over two hours.

Fearing I might not survive, the doctors took me immediately to surgery. My uncle, a doctor on the hospital staff, located the best possible surgeon. Fortunately, he was available on short notice. The renowned orthopedic specialist acted quickly to save me. "I did something that I tell my students never to do," he told me later. "I put a dirty bone back in your leg wound. I had to do it to save your life," he said. For years, he worked with me, continuing to use his expertise to preserve my legs and my ability to use them.

Lindsay waited for us on the Bartlett's porch in Jefferson all afternoon. She heard about the near-fatal collision on the television evening news. She heard " one passenger was injured, the other might not live." She didn't know they were talking about her mother and brother.

My injuries, from head to toe, were so severe the family kept Lindsay from visiting during my first month in the hospital. They feared she'd be frightened by the awful way I looked. My parents

"Will I Be on Television?"

wrote the nuns at school and to Jane Bartlett. They described what happened and my hospitalization. The letter meant more to Lindsay than I imagined at the time. Many years later, she talked about Jane's reading it to her and how Jane "made me feel better."

When I'd recovered enough to turn my head to one side, my nurse would prop a pillow near my face and lay the phone on it. I was able to talk to Lindsay, and hear her familiar little lisp. It was comforting to listen to the encouraging words one of the sisters must have taught her to say, "You'll make it!"

Even at ten years, Lindsay rarely offered more than brief sentences or one word answers to questions. Nevertheless, my ability to speak with her eased my mind considerably. She seemed to flourish at St. Coletta's and with the Bartletts. I believed that she could have no real concept of the crash or my situation. She would know only that I wasn't visiting as often. She wouldn't worry, I thought, as long as I made regular calls.

After about six weeks flat on my back, when my head and shoulders could at last be propped up, my parents brought Lindsay to see me. In a favorite blue dress and wearing black patent leather shoes, she almost skipped into the room. She was that eager to see me—until she stopped short, staring. Had I been given a mirror, I would have understood why I'd frighten anyone. My face was still swollen. My eyes were black and blue. I must have looked like a cartoon of an injured skier, with my legs in white plaster casts from hip to ankle, strung up above the bed by chains.

No wonder Lindsay stared. When I tried to turn toward her, the chain anchoring one of my legs clattered against the metal traction frame that held it. The clinking noise scared her. Staring at both legs, she was uncertain. She hesitated to come near my bed.

I reached my hand out to her, but puzzled, she kept staring at my legs. She'd look away and back at them. From the vantage point of that tiny sprite, they must have looked like massive white pillars stretching to the sky. I searched for words to comfort her.

"My legs were hurt," I said. "The doctor is fixing them."

"Hurt?" Lindsay asked, coming slightly nearer my bed.

"They were hurt but they'll soon be all right," I said. "Held up like that, they'll get well." She was trying to understand.

"I'm glad to see you," I told her, hoping to change her mood and reassure her.

"Come closer so I can give you a hug."

"Does it hurt?"

"No," I lied. "The doctor is making them better."

Lindsay remained quiet during the rest of her visit and I was reassured. I believed that, no matter my physical situation, being with me again would ease her mind about my not being with her as often as before.

Rather than being concerned about Lindsay, my worries were about Bruce. I believed that Lindsay's mental age wasn't enough for her to be aware of the seriousness of the crash. I believed she was protected from its trauma by distance and by explanations she'd receive from Jane Bartlett and the nuns. Knowing the Bartletts and the nuns, I was certain of their kindness. They would help Lindsay deal with whatever worries or fears she might have.

Bruce was the one I was seriously worried about. I believed he was too young a boy to have suffered such severe trauma. I worried not only about his injuries and recovery. I worried about the rest of his life. Would dreams of the crash or unexpected reminders bring back frightful memories? I could not have been more wrong. In the case of both Lindsay and Bruce, what I believed at the time, and for years afterward, was the exact opposite of the truth.

It wasn't until I asked Lindsay about the crash, years later, that I learned the truth. She surprised me by remembering so clearly. Her answers were astounding.

"I was ten," she said. "Mrs. Bartlett read me a letter. You and Bruce were in an automobile crash. It was terrible. I felt terrible. I

"Will I Be on Television?"

was scared. I was petrified." She thought for a few minutes and added, "Mrs. Bartlett tried to make me feel better."

In 1962, at the time of the crash, there were not many studies about how children with special needs react to change. Dr. Susan Folstein, collaborating with my writing this book, taught me why I was so wrong to believe that Lindsay would not have a reaction to my being injured, to my extended stay in the hospital and to being out of immediate contact with her. I also learned how wrong I was not to open more of a discussion of my injuries the first time she saw me in the hospital.

Dr. Folstein told me, "Studies of children with special needs have documented their strong attachment to their mothers, even children with autism who are often assumed to have little attachment to their families when they are young. It is just the same for them, possibly worse, because any change in routine, or caregiver, can send them into a real tailspin of anxiety. They are almost abnormally closely attached to their mothers even though this is a strange sort of attachment. Some won't let their mothers out of their sight, even at night."

Anxiety is common in all children with special needs. They don't understand the world well enough to deal with the unexpected. Illness in a family member can send them into a panic. They may sleep poorly and develop nightmares.

Though Lindsay isn't autistic, these studies of attachment explain why she was so terribly frightened when she learned I was injured and in the hospital. They also explain why, even as an adult, no matter where she is or what she's doing, she calls me daily, just to be reassured.

Bruce, on the other hand, treated his six weeks in the hospital as an adventure. "Because everyone was so nice to me," he said. When hurled to the engine wall beneath the dashboard, he fractured his collarbone and nose. His leg was shattered by a compound fracture and in a similar kind of cast to mine. Following surgery, he was ambulatory and managed well on crutches. Bruce was a trouper. After several weeks, he visited me and handled my startling appearance quite well.

July passed for me in a haze of morphine. I slept, not wanting to awaken. For if the morphine wore off the excruciating pain was unbearable. When the heat of August arrived, with no air conditioning and only one open window, the nurses worked to keep me comfortable. I'd awaken to see flowers filling the room and get-well cards pinned on the walls. Angels in nurses' uniforms encouraged me. My children's need of me propelled me to get well. Otherwise, I could easily have given up. My private duty nurse, Barbara, was angel-in-chief. Years later I can still remember her voice saying, "see him," and my quickly glancing at a stranger, striding determinedly past the open door to my hospital room. "Two months ago he was worse than you are. Look at how he's walking now," she said, "If he can walk like that, you can do it, too." I believed her.

Whether I still believe that what Barbara said was true or whether the man was someone who happened to walk by at that moment doesn't matter. Using that man as a model gave me the determination I needed to be able to walk again. I believed that if he could do what Barbara told me he could do, I could do it, too.

As soon as I sufficiently recovered to be more presentable, the family brought Bruce, on his crutches, and Lindsay to visit again. It was immediately obvious to everyone that Lindsay visibly relaxed when we were together. She was sweet and sympathetic, mainly wanting to know when I'd be home again and, "Can I come to visit?" She asked the same question many times. The more times I told her "yes" and described what we'd do together at home, the happier she became.

"Will I Be on Television?"

Cary was my most frequent visitor, brought by the family or friends and neighbors. The day of the crash, Cary was staying out-of-town with her good friend, Polly, Betty's daughter. She remained, living with that family for over a month. We didn't see each other because of the distance to the hospital, but she called almost daily to talk to my nurse. Eventually, I was able to talk to her myself.

Friends in Minneapolis were in touch with flowers and cards. Several traveled to visit as I recuperated. Don made no effort to contact me or the children after we moved away. He came to the hospital once. When my nurse asked if I wanted to see him I told her, "No!"

In addition to Bruce's and my recuperating, Lindsay's well-being and Cary's taking on many of my household chores, there was another major concern. I didn't know how I'd pay our medical costs without insurance coverage from the driver who caused the injuries. Fortunately, our miracles hadn't run their course. The collision took place on a Monday. The driver purchased her car the preceding Friday. Her three-day earlier purchase meant the car still carried the car dealer's license plates. Financially, that was fortuitous. Generally, uninsured motorist clauses were not included in policies. My policy would cover only if I were at fault. Though the other driver had no insurance to cover extensive medical expenses, the dealer and his insurance company were held legally responsible.

"My Name is Lins"

Word of the crash and the news of my condition raced throughout our town like the game of Telephone. One tells one who tells another, who tells another, 'til most of the town is sharing the news. Unexpectedly, we were wrapped in a blanket of kindness. My room was turned into a flower garden, with baskets of blossoms filling every niche and window sill. A woman I never met sent an exquisite bouquet of tea roses and we became lifelong friends.

Floral gifts were held high for me to admire as I lay prone on my back, not permitted to so much as raise my head. Their beauty and delicate fragrance soothed my waking hours. One wall was papered with "get well" cards, also tacked high. There's no doubt that this overwhelming love and affection helped me to bear the excruciating pain, long days and sleepless nights.

During my hospitalization, Lindsay was being carefully prepared for leaving the Bartlett's home and becoming a boarding student at St. Coletta's. In the normal course of events, new students at the school lived with a selected family in Jefferson for about a year, in order to become acclimated to life away from their home. Having the stability of family life at the start made the transition from home to school much easier for the younger ones. It also gave the school staff an opportunity to assess the child's ability to adjust. Lindsay's advisor thought she was ready to make the move.

Until the day Lindsay visited me in the hospital, I'd agreed with the advisor's timing for her move to the school. Seeing her fear of my incapacitation, I had second thoughts. Wouldn't it be better for her to have the security of Jane Bartlett and her family while I was in the hospital? For several weeks I mulled over the pros and cons, a mulling process that seemed all-too-frequent whenever I had to make a decision of changing circumstances for Lindsay. No decision was ever quick or easy.

Considering that Lindsay didn't have the stability of our family, Lindsay's advisor and Jane Bartlett, with whom she was living, favored postponement, as I did. The only one whose opinion we didn't ask was Lindsay. At ten years she was unable to put her feelings into words. She spoke little, placidly cooperating with whatever course was set for her, rarely voicing an opinion. At times I sensed her wishes. Most times it was necessary to rely on my judgment or that of her caregivers.

Had anyone asked Lindsay, we would have known she was looking forward to living in the *big girls'* dormitory. She was not only ready for the move, but eager. Eventually, when she became a boarder she adjusted immediately and thrived, living at school with her new friends.

As Lindsay has grown, I've pondered the reason I may not have given weight to what was really on her mind. She wasn't able to express her opinions or emotions, as her siblings did, so I didn't make the necessary effort to delve into her unspoken wishes. I didn't give credit to her perception or her emotional intelligence. I regret that I let her disability set the pace and never probed further. There were too many lost years before I learned to help my daughter share her opinions. Not until Lindsay was a teenager did I realize she had a mind of her own. It wasn't until she furiously emphasized to me, over and over again, "I want to make my own decisions," that I finally got the message.

"Will I Be on Television?"

After four months of confinement in my hospital bed I felt as if I was in prison. Despair took over. Though the pain eased and I'd learned to sleep on my back, I could no longer endure not being able to change positions and badly needed evidence of becoming normal again. I pleaded with the doctors to let me go home. They remained hesitant because the crushed bones in my left thigh hadn't knitted together. My leg needed more time to heal and extended physical therapy was necessary before I could put any weight on that leg.

My surgeon understood and finally agreed to my leaving the hospital, but with the caveat that I would do the necessary exercises at home, in order to create what he called a "union" in my left leg. His instructions were that I was not to attempt to stand or put weight on my legs. After one month, I was to return to the hospital for physical therapy. He explained what I had to do at home and said, "We'll know there's a union of your thigh and lower leg when you can lift your leg off the bed without someone lifting it for you." That exercise turned out to be like trying to lift a load of iron with a weakened leg. But when he described it, I had no idea of the difficulty and readily agreed.

To celebrate my release I had my first shampoo in four months and that night I was taken out-of-doors in a wheelchair to see the glory of the full moon. It was like stepping into a world I'd never seen. Diffused beams of the moon's light softened the entire landscape. The air was filled with the crisp fresh fragrance of October's falling leaves. A gentle zephyr rippled my hair. I felt the astounding wonder of being alive.

In those unforgettably moving moments, I believed I understood what really matters in life. It is to be alive to appreciate the beauty of the natural gifts of our universe, too often taken for granted, yet constantly there, free for every one of us to savor whenever we wish. For that short time, all worries about my legs and concerns for the future were forgotten.

Extraordinary was the day I arrived home in an ambulance. I was greeted by a wide white banner across the front of our house, reading WELCOME HOME JAN. Led by Bruce, a crowd of nearly forty friends and neighbors covered the lawn from the curb to the front porch. Inside the house food overflowed the dining table and kitchen counters. Perhaps I should have been weary from the long drive. Instead, I felt rejuvenated and thrilled.

Several weeks later, when the family believed I was stable enough to handle the information, I was told the details of the crash. The four-door Oldsmobile that hit us weighed more than a ton. It was much older, larger and far heavier than my light-weight Lark. I was told that I'd managed to get our car off the road and into the ditch that hugged the road's shoulder, except for the driver's side front wheel. The Oldsmobile followed us and crashed head-on into our Lark in the ditch on that part of the car. As pictured starkly in photographs taken at the scene, our car was so severely telescoped and crunched into pieces that it was hard to understand how either Bruce or I survived. When I saw the pictures, I had trouble processing the horror of what happened.

The woman driver of the other car was released from that hospital after only a few days. Five children in the back seat of the other car were thrown about from the impact. Only one was badly hurt, though they were all taken to the same hospital as Bruce. Bruce became friendly with the boy who was in the hospital for three weeks before being released. Bruce was hospitalized for a month and was still using crutches when he was discharged.

It also became important to sort out problems caused by the crash. In addition to Bruce's and my injuries, Lindsay's adjustment at school and the children needing reassurance that eventually I'd be all right, there were other issues. Who would care

"Will I Be on Television?"

for us during my month at home? How would we manage if I couldn't walk soon and couldn't work? How would I pay our mounting medical costs? The woman driver of the car that hit us was uninsured.

That's when more miracles began. An attorney, who lived just across our backyard offered to handle our case. He investigated enough to learn that the Oldsmobile, purchased only three days before the collision, still carried the car dealer's license plates. He obtained a court order making the dealer responsible for selling the car to an uninsured driver. The result was that the dealer's insurer would compensate us for our costs.

To solve another of our problems, a family in the neighborhood had an elderly Aunt Cathy offering help as the caretaker we needed at home. But we were warned that Aunt Cathy could be cranky and crotchety. Other neighbors tactfully suggested we look elsewhere.

So, my family's search began, but they weren't prepared for what they encountered. In the 60's there were no available avenues for seeking temporary home care, except from one's own family or the church bulletin that carried rare notices of household help. Doors quietly closed if a child with special needs was involved. It didn't matter that Lindsay lived away at St. Coletta's, we seemed to be the only ones appreciating our delightful little girl.

Had I a time machine that could turn the clock forward three decades, a solution would have been at hand. In the 80's and 90's parents of children with special needs began companies of caregivers to meet individual in-home requirements. But it took almost fifty years, and the Internet, to be offered what would have been at the top of our wish list in the 60's.

If my time machine turned to the present, it would find a number of firms offering specialized home care. In 2012, not only does one company provide help for special needs, such help is specifically titled, "Autism Care Considerations," and "Down Syndrome Care." A care seeker, invited to enter the appropriate information on the the Internet, would receive a specific caregiver's work history, biography and available days and times and references.

In one state an organization offers respite care, defining "respite" as "getting a break from the responsibilities of being a parent." Without specifically describing the "constantly on-hand twenty-four-hours-a-day" parent of a child with special needs, this firm offers "needed relief, an essential survival tool."

The caretaker team approach grew as professionals and caregivers formed teams to meet the child's and parent's specific needs such as health, education, psychological, or simply time off. The Internet became an excellent tool in the search for help. Costs differed according to individual requirements. Some states began to offer Human Resources financial aid.

In the 60's, since there was no aid of this kind, we accepted Aunt Cathy's cranky and crochety services with gratitude. She surprised everyone by turning into a kindly saint who took pity on our predicament and responded to our fighting spirit.

Lindsay soon came home for a long weekend. We were a family together again. Constantly on the go, the children made the most of her visit. Lindsay, of course, was in the midst of the activity. More than comfortable with Cary and Bruce, she was still tentative with me. I attempted many times to reach out to her, without understanding her concern. It wasn't until years later that I was told trauma can affect a child with special needs because it affects their routine or their expectations. As simple an event as a parent not coming when expected takes on seriousness for them.

As I watched and enjoyed the children's fun from my wheel chair, I might have realized that seeing me in a wheelchair troubled Lindsay. It wasn't the way she was used to seeing me. It

"Will I Be on Television?"

was the first time, but not the last, that she asked, "Are you my real mother?"

Her mind was off me when the other two directed her in kitchen chores, issuing instructions like army sergeants teaching the newest private. But with a budding sense of humor she teased back as they teased her. Replays of those scenes became family vignettes, told and retold to this day.

One day, Lindsay firmly announced, "My name is Stephanie," never explaining her reason for adopting the new name. During her next visit home, she was Lindsay again, but this time she added a middle name and suffix. She was Lindsay-Louise-A-Third. Maybe a boy at school had the Roman numeral III after his name, causing him to be George Johnson III, or George Johnson, the third. We tried to explain this to Lindsay with little success. Lindsay remained A-Third, providing us many laughs with our Lindsay-A-Third joining in the laughter. After trying on a number of other names Lindsay settled on Lins and Lins it is to this day. If someone strays, they will, promptly— and— sternly, be corrected with, "My name is Lins."

Her adjustment to dormitory life tickled us in other ways, primarily with her descriptions of dorm and school activities. For instance, in classes she studied "drawers" and "tables. To an observer at school, these words would translate to arranging her clothes neatly in a wardrobe and being taught table manners. "Nightime" to Lindsay meant learning to bathe herself, brush her teeth and sleep quietly in a dormitory with her schoolmates. She described her many new friends in simple terms, such as "his hair is red," or "I like Sally" but "John makes noise." The accuracies of her descriptions were borne out when we met the children she described.

Often a source of comment is Lindsay's guileless honesty. Just as with her descriptions, she will offer information or opinion in few words, right to the point. Those who know my daughter also know that whether information is complimentary or critical, she shares it with no qualms. About Lindsay, we often hear laughter, followed by "Lindsay tells it just the way it is." Her known inability to keep a secret was used by Cary and Bruce to find hidden birthday and Christmas gifts. With active children, Lindsay one of them, our family life became a three-ring-circus during her visits.

Thanksgiving also arrived during that first month home. With my leg straight out in front on the wheelchair extension, I couldn't baste the usual celebratory bird. Instead, we roasted a standing rib of beef, with no requirements other than an oven. Adorned with my crayon drawing of a turkey, that Lindsay colored brown while the others added feathers, that roast became the only "Thanksgiving turkey" to earn a place in the family history book.

November also was Lindsay's time to practice for St. Coletta's Christmas pageant. In white organza, wearing a halo, she would be an angel in the play. Our adorable angel was quite a contrast to the imp we knew. I so wanted to be in the audience to see her.

I redoubled my efforts to create a 'union' in my left leg. The recipe for success was to lie flat on my back with a pillow propping my head and to be able to raise my left foot from the bed. It took laser-like concentration to revive muscles I no longer had. It took herculean effort, both mentally and physically. Each day I worked harder during two or three half-hour sessions. But I couldn't get my foot off the bed. With only four days before I had to return to the hospital I thought I'd have to give up, but miraculously and against all odds, two days later I succeeded. My leg was *two inches* above the mattress!

I kept my promise to return to the hospital after the month at home. Aunt Cathy stayed with the children. Hospitalized again, I had intensive therapy, but I was still was not permitted to put weight on my left leg. The surgeon called the bone above my

"Will I Be on Television?"

knee "gravel." After three weeks, while getting ready to go home, he handed me this staggering blow, "Unless you have additional surgery to take bone from your hip and transplant it to your left leg, you won't walk again." The shock of having to face more surgery after what I'd just been through was like being hit with a baseball bat. It made my mind go blank for some minutes.

"How long will it take?" I had to know.

"It will be the same as this time." The thought of four more months in bed, not able to move, was unbearable.

"Four months?" He nodded his head, yes.

"Can you assure good results?"

"The success of the surgery can't be assured." He said, "I'm sorry."

I'd been so certain I was over the worst. I was making progress. Instead, the doctor was telling me that if I didn't go through the next step, I'd be crippled and in a wheel chair for the rest of my life.

Then he said, "Don't stand or put any weight on that leg." Then he added, "If you fall or damage your leg you will never walk again."

My future shattered in pieces. I longed to be out in the sun, running, playing with my children, again riding the horse I'd been training the morning before the crash. A second long hospital stay was more than I could endure. How would Cary and Bruce get along without me for four months? How could my diminished bank account handle the cost of more surgery and Aunt Cathy? On the other hand, what would happen to my children if I could never walk again? If I couldn't work? It took money for Lindsay to remain at St. Coletta's. What if I couldn't afford to keep her there and couldn't take care of her at home? What would happen to her?

"I Got Lost in the Chicago Airport"

The timing was all wrong for whatever decision I made. Thanksgiving had eased into preparations for Christmas, and I saw no need to spoil the 'happiest season of all' by bringing up the choices that faced me. One was worse than the next. There would be time after the holidays to face the reality of my physical problem and my family's future.

Boxes of Christmas tree ornaments, tinsel and garlands spilled from the attic and littered the living room carpet. Traditions and happy memories always made the holidays a special time. From my wheelchair or the living room couch, I could play a part in the flurry and fun of being home. The only immediate disappointment was the looming date of Lindsay's Christmas pageant. Unable to walk, I'd miss watching her perform as the angel she'd announced herself to be. Rarely was I alone. But one afternoon at dusk no one else was home. Cary and Bruce were at a neighborhood Christmas party. Lindsay was at school. Aunt Cathy was shopping. Relaxing on the living room couch, admiring our trimmed and lighted tree across the room, I mused about a Christmas story I'd heard years before. It was about a fully trimmed Christmas tree. No matter how many different kinds of gimmicks the family tried to make their tree remain standing, it would tip and fall. An engineer, the story teller, strung out the tale 'til the audience was laughing hilariously. He made quite a show of the solution. "How did they miss the bent trunk?"

A straight trunk could have borne the weight with no problem. I started wondering, *Would that same principal apply to my walking if I didn't bend my knee?* With a long pause to decide whether or not I should take a forbidden gamble, I put my bare feet on the carpet and straightened my leg as much as possible. I stood for a minute to balance and test my leg's weight bearing. Slowly, I took thirteen steps to our Christmas tree and thirteen back to the sofa. My leg didn't buckle. Straight legged, I tried again to make sure it worked. I walked!

For nearly two weeks I kept the secret. I needed no doubters to warn I might fall. Each time I was alone at home I'd try again and succeed. For too long I'd lost control of the simplest activities, going where I wanted to go and getting somewhere when I wanted to. Those awkward first steps gave me a new appreciation for Lindsay's pluck when she attempted walking. I wondered, too, if she'd shared the same exhilaration when success was assured.

Soon I'd practiced enough to show my family and the doctors that I could walk again without harm. I wouldn't need more surgery. It was the most glorious gift of my Christmas. The surgeon's words, "had you damaged your leg by those attempts to walk, I never could have repaired it," had me realizing how blessed I was. A few weeks later, walking safely with a metal walker, I was able to see Lindsay in her Christmas pageant.

With much preparation to get there we were almost late. We didn't have a chance to be with Lindsay before she was onstage. As the lights dimmed, my parents, Cary, Bruce and I were ushered down the aisle of the school's packed auditorium. Our seats were in the first row so I wouldn't have to bend my knee a lot in order to be seated.

Onstage, the delightful voices of the school's choir were introducing the manger scene. A shining star spotlighted the children gathered around the scene of baby Jesus' birth. The children, as woolly lambs in adorable handmade costumes, carefully milled about a young Virgin Mary who knelt near a rough-hewn

"Will I Be on Television?"

wooden cradle. The next scene brought onstage three magnificently costumed tiny wise men, clothed in multi-colored brocade. They bore golden chests of gifts for the Christ child. All the while a chorus of young voices, behind the scenes, provided the joyous music of Christmas.

As the chorus began "Hark the Herald Angels Sing," it became St. Coletta's littlest angels' turn to perform. In flowing white organza, a sparkling halo and feathered wings slightly askew, Lindsay appeared with nine other miniature angels, all dressed in the same flowing white. A leader angel attempted to gather the little girls into what was meant to be a precise dance line. She wasn't immediately successful. One small angel had to be turned to face the audience. Another bent to tie her dragging shoelace. A third ran from behind the pulled-back curtain to catch up to the others.

Our eyes were on Lindsay as the line took the shape it was supposed to be. At the exact mid-point of the lineup Lindsay looked poised and as proud as one could be, giving new meaning to the words "Center Stage." As Lindsay stood there her eyes were busy. She saw us.

Unrehearsed and obviously unplanned, our special angel broke out of the line. With her feather wings flapping she scooted to the front of the stage and stood there waving vigorously. The audience's barely muffled laughter rang out as the leader angel darted out of the line and grabbed Lindsay's hand, pulling her back to her proper place. She straightened Lindsay's toppling halo as the dance music began. My daughter's beatific smile of proud innocence, as she performed her steps, made it clear that she'd *never* think of herself as a fallen angel.

―•―•◆•―•◆•―•―

When life was back to normal after the holidays and despite the success of my walking and the frequent recounting of Lindsay's "*stardom*," there was a frightening road ahead. Shortly, we'd be out of money. Reimbursement for our medical costs wouldn't happen any time soon. Though our attorney proved the car dealer was responsible for a large settlement, a trial was essential and might be a year away. Not surprisingly, the insurance company found reasons for delays.

In addition, Don's monthly checks, never certain, began to come irregularly. More court action on that score might be necessary. Never before had I faced the prospect of mounting late payments, debt and wondering where money would come from. Particularly, I worried about Lindsay. If I couldn't afford to pay St. Coletta's tuition, would she have to live at home without the preparation for her years of challenges ahead? How does a mother alone, with three children, one handicapped, solve financial crises? As I began to know other parents at Lindsay's school, I discovered that many had similar problems.

For families with handicapped children financial questions can be profound. Many go through periods of severe financial struggle. Far too many can't find the money needed for their child's care. Extra costs for a challenged child will affect the entire family's standard of living. Siblings may be deprived of necessities, of college education or career training.

In the 60s few options were available. It was uncommon for a single parent to work regularly while caring for a challenged child in the home. Years later, as Special Needs became publicly acknowledged, accompanying financial problems were recognized. In forerunner states, families became eligible for government benefits. Charitable school and training programs were started. Much later, after years of technological advances, the Internet became a tool for seeking help. Media focus on increasing autism and other mental disabilities brought with it increasing aid for all Special Needs. Even so, the need remains greater than the resources available.

"Will I Be on Television?"

When we were most in need, no public or private financial help was available for our family. But just at the time I felt most despondent about our future a second Christmas gift took shape. A favorite aunt urged me to move to the East Coast of the United States where she lived. She assured me of fine public schools for the children, cutting-edge medical care for me and the possibility of locating a placement similar to St. Coletta's for Lindsay.

My aunt's suggestion of aid came at the best possible time, helping to take our minds off immediate problems and allowing us to look forward to new adventure. Moving east was a perfect solution. My aunt's first two assurances, fine schools and excellent medical help proved correct.

But searching for a suitable school for Lindsay hit a dead end. St. Coletta's was the rare school of its kind. It was just right for Lindsay. While very reluctant to leave her far from us, an airline program provided a tolerable solution. Lindsay would fly home as "an unaccompanied minor." It meant Lindsay would fly with an attendant in charge of her during the flight. Upon arrival she'd be placed directly in my care.

At eleven Lindsay was better able to understand and manage. She was comfortable traveling alone, as long as someone stood by if she needed help. She was friendly with strangers. Too friendly, perhaps. Throughout the flight her seatmate might be forced to be entertained by her entire life story. I met one or two who not only didn't mind, they told me how much they enjoyed her company.

Still, like every mother, I was nervous about Lindsay's flying cross-country by herself. What if a mistake was made? What if she were left alone and someone took advantage of her because of her handicap? I rationalized my concerns and began to plan our move to the East. Always, when we were together, I talked with

Lindsay about our not seeing each other as often. As was her habit at that age she didn't question. "You'll be having the fun of flying on an airplane to our new home," I'd tell her often.

"Airplane," she'd say, excitedly. She seemed to understand that while we may not be with each other as often, she would love the adventure of flying.

At school, I talked with the Sisters about our plans. Sister Mary Clare offered to drive Lindsay to the airport for her flights home and to meet her when she returned. My aunt's gifts made it affordable for her to fly home every three months and be with us for at least two weeks. Her first time home would be three weeks after we moved. When we counted the days together on her fingers, she held them up excitedly to show me. "Days," she said.

After her first flight and several more successful flights, my fears for her well-being were eased. I was reassured by airline attendants who told me she was cooperative and had a sense of humor on the plane. "She's a friendly chatterbox," one said. Always eager to fly, she had happy experiences. She was tickled by the nickname we gave her, "Queen of the Skies."

At times I was permitted to meet her at the end of the plane's ramp when she arrived. Other times I'd be kept away from the gate and stood where I could see far down the exit walkway. She'd see me at a distance and know I was there for her. Waiting after one flight, I watched as all the other passengers came through the gate. The walkway was deserted and still no Lindsay. Alarmed, I looked around for anyone I could find in an airline uniform, so I could ask them about my daughter.

Just then, I saw a group of pilots and attendants walking toward me from the plane, talking animatedly. Imagining the worst, I neared panic.

"*Something must have happened to Lindsay*, I thought frantically. *That's why they're all talking.* Then I saw a small someone in the midst of the group. There was Lindsay, looking like a tiny doll in her blue coat and blue bonnet, wearing shiny black patent leather slippers and white anklets. Enraptured by their attention, she was smiling from ear to ear. When they approached me, one of the pilots said, "Lindsay is our new best friend," passing to me her little hand that he'd been holding. After a few introductions and greetings, the group left. As they walked on, each person turned around, waved and called, "Goodbye Lindsay."

From then on, I did nothing but brag about how Lindsay enjoyed flying, how successfully she flew "all the way across the country by herself," and how she *ordered* from us "two new *luggages* for Christmas."

"Don't you worry about her?" a friend asked during one of her visits home years later, when Lindsay was at my side. Lindsay's handicap is obvious because of her small size and sometimes bland facial expression, prompting similar questions from time to time. Folks were surprised and impressed with her ability despite her challenges.

"Not at all," I answered. "She handles herself and her flights very well. I'm really proud of her. The airline attendants protect her," I said, beaming with pride and continuing to enlarge on my glowing comments. All the while Lindsay didn't say a word, until she confounded not only the friend I was talking to, but me as well.

"What about that time I got lost in the Chicago airport?" she announced.

"You did what?" I completely lost my composure.

"I got lost in the Chicago airport," she said.

"When?"

"When I got off the plane when I wasn't supposed to."

"How long were you lost?"

"I don't know. You told me not to get off the plane but I did."

"Did you get off when other passengers got off?"

"When other passengers got off," she said.

"Who found you?"

"I don't know."

"Weren't you frightened? I asked.

"Yes," she said matter-of-factly. Never afraid to face a challenge, she reported this with her usual equanimity.

I was the one that had to calm down for I was busy imagining the evils that might have beset her while she was alone in a monstrously huge airport. Still, I couldn't picture Lindsay crying, panicky, or letting anyone know of her fear. Instead, I pictured her waiting patiently until someone came to her rescue. Partly, that would be because of her innocence. Equally, it would be because of her courage.

My lesson learned from this? It was the importance of anticipating the unexpected. I'd concentrated on keeping my daughter protected always, by myself or others. At eleven years, it was necessary to prepare her for taking care of herself in an emergency. Though, at that moment my thoughts were mostly on the courage of the child holding tight to my hand while we talked.

A Decision Dilemma

In mid-year we moved east; soon to discover the exhilarating dynamic of living only an hour from Manhattan, coupled with a warm welcome by members of a suburban "bedroom" community. Virtually adopted by the neighbors, my children and I soon made new friends. For Cary and Bruce, we soon learned that the public school teachers in our small community were at the level of excellence we'd been seeking.

Less than a month after we were settled, Lindsay flew cross-country to see her new home. In the 60s the stigma of a 'mentally retarded' child was pervasive. Rather than have Lindsay stared at, possibly teased or hurt, I kept her busy at home. I didn't encourage her to meet or play outside with the other neighborhood children. I hated giving in to prejudice, but it seemed best way to handle a situation that could turn into a problem.

At the same time, it was good to see that nothing had changed in the relationship with her siblings. To them, Lindsay's lack of ability didn't matter a whit. Cary and Bruce welcomed her visit and the four of us had our usual great times. We fiercely competed at games, chose straws for who would be head-chef during cooking sessions and invited to dinner those close friends who knew about Lindsay's challenges. We took excursions to New York and other nearby tourist sites where Lindsay blended into the crowds. Strangers would look questioningly at her, but she was too innocent and having much too much fun to notice.

Where had the years gone? Lindsay would soon approach her twelfth year. Year after year, for eleven and counting, I'd been held in the vise-like grip of indecision. I had sole responsibility for the life or death of my daughter Lindsay.

Lindsay was born with a heart valve that didn't close as it should. The problem was common enough to have a name, patent ductus arteriosus. Surgery to close the duct would be necessary, but her pediatrician thought it wisest to delay until she was older.

I remember our conversation clearly. I was in his office, sitting in a comfortable leather lounge chair across from his desk. Through his window, the spring sun brightend his office, touching a corner of his desk and the arm of my chair.

Describing the surgery, he said, "It's not dangerous, but it's better for her to have it when she's older. Meanwhile, it shouldn't cause a problem." He described the operation and time in the hospital in more detail, adding, "But she must have the surgery before she's twelve years old. If she doesn't have it her heart will eventually run down."

I can't recall the questions I asked before he clarified his answers by adding, "If she doesn't have the surgery, she won't live past twenty years or twenty-one." He emphasized that sentence, saying it twice. He said, "Compare her heart to a clock that needs winding. If it isn't wound, it will stop."

Given the usual circumstances, the average child with the same problem would have the necessary surgery when old enough to understand and handle it physically. That day, I believed Lindsay would have the operation when she was somewhere between eight and ten. The doctor made it sound simple. I wasn't worried.

But from nine months on, Lindsay was no longer an average child. Over time, as Lindsay grew and adapted to her disability, I'd ask different doctors the same question, "Should we think about her heart surgery?" Though her general health was excellent, advice against the surgery continued to be unanimous.

"Will I Be on Television?"

I knew that, as a rule, disabled children lived shorter lives than the norm. But I couldn't help wondering if the doctors' decision would be the same if Lindsay were not disabled. As my daughter thrived, indecision hung over me like a dark cloud. Could I put Lindsay through the surgery? Still, how could I let my child be debilitated and die at a young age if it could be prevented?

For Lindsay, as an intellectually challenged person there were other ramifications. In terms of her future as a disabled adult in a prejudiced world, what would happen to her if I were no longer around? What if the only solution available was institutional?

Considering everything I knew, my decision came down to—*Was a short happy life for Lindsay better than a long difficult one? Should I be judge and jury? Should I play God?* Making what I understood as a life or death decision for my daughter, was something I couldn't face. While there was still time left, I procrastinated. Lindsay flew back to St. Coletta's.

———◆·ı◆ı·◆·———

Cary adapted to her new school quickly. Soon elected a class officer she also earned a high honor during her junior and senior year. Each year the members of the Girls Athletic Association divided themselves into two teams. They competed by presenting a mini-Broadway show. The best show won. A mark of Cary's junior classmates' regard was being elected co-captain of the Orange team. Only two girls were elected each year, one for Orange and one co-captain for the Blue team. The junior co-captain became captain of her team in her senior year. Cary's devotion to her Orange team became a family affair. There were countless meetings in our home for conceiving the production, painting scenery, gathering costumes and props. The girls created a melodrama for the show, with all of its dramatic twists and turns. Included was the heroine, Cary, tied to onstage tracks with a train bearing down.

When the Orange team won, students, parents and the town celebrated with great banners, horn-honking car parades and late night parties. As captain of the record breaking Orange team, Cary was presented with one of the school's most prestigious awards and a bright orange banner hid the front of our house for weeks.

———•◆•┃◆┃•◆•———

Still recuperating, but improving, I answered a call for a volunteer position at a nearby state-run mental health institution. Shortly thereafter, I was invited to direct a program for volunteers that trained them in counseling patients. Following eighteen months of my in-service training as a psychiatric social worker, I was offered a permanent position at the hospital and given access to areas outside my office that I hadn't previously inspected.

The campus of the hospital where I worked was far different from that of the gray concrete, barred windowed institutions I'd seen in 1953, the year Lindsay was born. Handsome red brick buildings, scattered over an acre of manicured lawns, didn't seem nearly as forbidding. Though what I found in the interior of the adult women's building, where most of my patients lived, was a stark and startling contrast.

All three floors lacked the barest essentials. Lavatory mirrors were broken glass; cracks were deep, pieces were missing. Stall doors were removed from their hinges. Toilet seats were non-existent as was toilet tissue. As soon as the tissue was distributed in the lavatories it was squirreled away by individual patients, in order for them to have any at all when it was needed.

Worn gray metal chairs, with hard seats and no arms, were the day room's only furnishings, except for a small television hung high up on a wall. The entire atmosphere was the most appalling and depressing I'd ever encountered. Would this have been the kind of place doctors envisioned for Lindsay when they recommended institutionalizing her?

"Will I Be on Television?"

Fifteen foot high windows were so covered with dirt one couldn't see out. The patients, themselves, reflected the atmosphere. Apathetic and unkempt, they'd long since lost most of their interest in personal care. Who could blame them? Nothing in their surroundings encouraged them to get well.

Nevertheless, dedicated doctors, specialist medical teams and staff members strived for the patients' progress and recovery. A slim state budget caused understaffing, resulting in long hours and making the staff's duties overly demanding. Even so, every colleague with whom I worked gave more than 100% of their skill, effort and time against those overpowering odds. Volunteers also pitched in to help the patients.

Volunteers read to them, walked with them and enlisted their participation in their healing process. Aided by staff members, Volunteers initiated a project of upgrading the women's building. Improvements took place over time, little by little.

Change in the patients' behavior followed, slow step by slow step. Hesitantly, the women began to talk among themselves. A few formed small groups. Some pulled up chairs to watch as the formerly streaked battleship gray walls were painted. Some were orange. Some were yellow and bright green. The painters were male patients who lived in a building across the courtyard. Some of the men climbed high ladders to wash the windows. Extra funds from the state were sought by staff members to equip the women with needed health and grooming supplies. As combs, toothbrushes and toiletries were distributed, the women became more receptive to improving their appearance.

Lavatories were cleaned and repaired by the hospital's maintenance team. Attractive, comfortably cushioned, mahogany couches and chairs were donated by a volunteer whose family owned a furniture store. They replaced the ugly and uncomfortable metal dayroom furniture. Volunteers planned an Inauguration Day celebration of the vastly improved surroundings. One long-term patient's touching behavior made the event unforgettable.

Amid a sizable group filled with anticipation, the ribbon across the door of the newly decorated and furnished dayroom was cut. In a fresh dress, combed hair, and wearing neatly applied lipstick, a formerly disheveled and disinterested woman walked across the room to one of the new chairs. Nearing it, she turned her back to the chair to carefully seat herself. With a lingering glance around the room to those watching, she made the lady-like gesture of reaching behind herself to smooth her new skirt before she sat down. She hadn't forgotten how to do so. Seating herself with a restored quiet dignity and a serene smile on her face, she politely folded her hands in her lap. A beautiful, unforgettable, moment was created for every one of us who understood her unspoken appreciation.

From that time on, with counseling, a number of the women improved and were able to return to their homes. Surprisingly, some who improved enough to leave were patients who had been in the hospital for many years.

Following my on-site training under a staff member holding a Doctorate of Social Work degree, I was awarded a scholarship for the Masters' Degree of Social Work program at Rutgers University. I continued working at the hospital and commuted thirty-five miles each way for classes three days a week.

My increase in income also helped. Cary entered college, where she took a job to lessen her costs. Bruce and I managed with household expenses cut to the bone. The insurance reimbursement continued to be delayed. The company was fighting payment. From my own over-burdened financial experience I learned to admire single-parent families. A single parent carries mother's and father's responsibilities for bringing up children. They are the bookkeeper, housekeeper, cook, chauffeur and, in my case, student and employed social worker who managed homework and answered patients' phone calls at night. At best, single parent life can be exhausting.

Still, I was more fortunate than many who had a child with special needs. I had the benefit of St. Coletta's school for Lindsay. I had doctors to consult about the impending and impossible decision about her heart surgery. Since most advised against it and I was uncertain, it was easy to procrastinate making a definite decision.

My son and I joined forces to make the best of our still slim financial condition. One freezing afternoon in winter, Bruce came home about five o'clock. It was already dark. Stamping snow from his feet and clapping his mittens together to warm his hands, he shed clumps of snow onto the kitchen floor. Holding out one frosty mitten, filled with a handful of wet crumpled bills and clinking coins, he offered me the weekly collection from his paper route. With a worried expression on his cold and reddened eleven-year-old face, he said. "Here Mom, take this, you and I have to keep Lindsay at St. Coletta's and Cary in college." Tears of tenderness fell as I hugged him.

The worst time was when Don refused to send a necessary check for Cary's semester registration at college because he'd bought a new car. After paying for Cary's fees and books, I didn't have enough money left to pay the electric bill. The electric company threatened to shut off our power. Somehow, the three of us didn't lose our sense of humor or the optimism of Lindsay's favorite expression, "*we'll make it*," even in the dark.

Despite our problems, I'd determined to scrape together thirty-five dollars to buy a puppy for Bruce, who was devastated by the death of a collie he'd adored from puppyhood. Our beloved Snowflake had to be put to sleep because of the infirmities of old age. At a distant kennel we found another lovable collie that we brought home. Grocery shopping one night for dog food for his new collie, Bruce and I purchased several extra-large bags of the kibbles and nothing else. Watching us quizzically as she rang our order, the checkout clerk turned to whisper to a co-worker. She didn't say anything to me or ask a question, so I paid little attention to her and put her action out of my mind.

The incident escaped my memory until a few days later, when I read the local newspaper. A featured heart-wrenching story was of a mother and son, so poor that she and her child were forced to buy dog food to eat. Bruce and I were sure the story meant us and found it something we could laugh about, though my heart went out to other families who might be living such a story.

Somehow we managed to stretch to make ends meet, and Lindsay was able to fly home at least three times a year. At work, I didn't talk about my special needs daughter, although during lunch at the hospital my colleagues and I often spoke of our children. Cynthia, who became a close friend, was one of the few who knew about Lindsay. I shared my excitement with her each time Lindsay flew home. Cynthia and I had worked together for almost two years, before the day she began our lunch break asking, "Have you been in all of the wards?"

"I'm not sure," I answered tentatively. The patients I worked with were primarily adult women, residing in the adult female building and I'd only been on the first floor of the male building.

"Have you been in a locked ward?" she continued.

"I didn't know there were locked wards," I said, surprised at her question.

"Very few are permitted in this one," she said. "Would you like to see it?"

With no further explanation, my friend cautioned that I might not like what I'd see. Curiosity made me say yes. Had I known what I'd find that afternoon, and be helpless to change, I've wondered if I would have reacted differently. Until that day, no one mentioned the ward. I had no idea it was part of the hospital.

"Will I Be on Television?"

After lunch Cynthia led me toward a two-story building, tucked in a valley behind similar buildings on the hospital grounds. Its red brick architecture was buried by bushy trees and shrubs; the hidden structure was nearly invisible. It blended completely into its surroundings. Cynthia took me to a roundabout narrow concrete walkway. The building had no imposing front door as did others on campus. We kept walking past the front, following stepping stones to an unobtrusive locked metal back door.

Cynthia fiddled with her key in the lock for a few minutes, before she could make it work. "Sometimes the key sticks," she said as she tugged to open the heavy door. We entered a dark, hot steamy hallway, where I became aware of a steady background sound, like children whimpering. Not a din, it was more a soft, constant dirge. The strong odor of urine permeated the air around us. Down a short hallway we entered a large room, empty of daylight save for what came through one small barred window in the concrete block wall and the door that was closing behind us. Bare dim ceiling bulbs shadowed the walls and floor. A child of about six years sat in a diaper, nothing else, on the bare stone floor near where we entered. She didn't look at us. Every few minutes, she banged her head against the concrete wall behind where she sat.

I started to go to her, until an attendant stepping from the shadows put an arm out to stop me. "We can't make her quit," she said. I couldn't stop watching that unfortunate little girl.

A number of painted white cribs in the room held small babies in skimpy diapers. The babies were uncovered because of the over-powering heat. They lay motionless on their backs, staring at the ceiling. The whimpering sound coming from the next room was louder as we walked toward it. The attendant left us, to go in that direction. I could hear voices in the room, but emotionally I was shaken and appalled. I had no desire to learn what I'd find. I'd seen enough.

I asked Cynthia to unlock the door we came through, to let me leave. Stepping outdoors, I gulped in the fresh air and sunshine as fast as I could. I was desparate for a balm to my soul. What I'd just witnessed could have been my daughter's fate had I followed the doctors' recommendation to institutionalize her? Was this how unwanted children were cared for in our supposedly civilized world?

That night, the dreadful experience helped me make the necessary decision about Lindsay's heart surgery. Unless attitudes changed, I didn't want to take a chance that my daughter might live a long life with anyone other than me making decisions for her. I decided that the question of whether or not to have Lindsay's surgery should be placed in the hands of God. Her twelfth birthday arrived, bringing with it her usual excitement and healthy vigor. But the story didn't end there.

"They Called Me Retard"

For six years Lindsay was sheltered and unaffected by the outside world, until the changing picture of mental health reached into St. Coletta's and snared her. About 1967, a concept called "mainstreaming" reached both public and private facilities that cared for the larger groups of residents with special needs. I became aware of it at the hospital where I worked before it affected Lindsay.

States began examining the rising costs of modernizing and maintaining out-of-date and over-crowded institutions. The concept of "mainstreaming" residents was introduced as both a solution and innovative progress. In our state psychiatric hospital, administrators, doctors and social workers were to concentrate on re-establishing the mentally ill in their homes and communities. Mental hospitals would gradually be emptied. Unfortunately, "mainstreaming" turned out to be another name for good intentions that boomeranged into unintended consequences. Too many patients had no families, no community ties. They were left stranded in large cities unable to fend for themselves.

For our hospital staff, it was a sad situation and a difficult one. Patients we'd worked with, and who had no capacity to care for themselves, were forced to be placed away from the hospital where some had lived for years. They floundered. The program was responsible for my nightly phone calls from those searching for support and help. Results of the "solution" are still seen in the homeless population of the nation.

Though St. Coletta's was a private school, its administration also adopted "mainstreaming" to some extent. Placement of the school's students was more successful than that of the state hospitals, because most students had families. It also was more gradual. Still, in too many cases what the child left behind in academics was of considerably greater benefit to them than alternative options offered by their home communities.

Unexpectedly, after being at St. Coletta's for six years, Lindsay was among those returned home. Perhaps it was because I was having difficulty keeping up with the tuition payments. Although scholarships had never been offered by the school, parents were permitted to pay what they could afford. Or, perhaps Mainstreaming was because of the 1965 St. Coletta Habilitation Program that was initiated to encourage young adults with mental retardation to become successful community members.

In 1983 the Kennedy family announced a gift in honor of Mrs. Rose Kennedy's 93rd birthday to facilitate a program that would serve as a national model for aging persons with mental retardation. St. Coletta's advanced with the times into other areas and now offers residential services. Recently renovated was St. Coletta's of Wisconsin's new corporate headquarters residing in the old Alverno building on the Jefferson campus. The Excel and Golden Options day programs are held in this building as well.

I was pleased to have my daughter living with us. The problem was what to do about her continuing education. She'd accomplished much at school, but at fourteen her intellectual level remained that of an eight-year-old.

Lindsay's best bet for help was the slowly improving public attitude toward the mentally challenged. Some public schools began to include early Special Education classes. One of those schools was the Middle School located in a neighboring suburb. Transportation would be a complication because the school bus didn't come to our town and my working hours barely permitted my driving her morning and afternoon. Nevertheless, enrolling Lindsay was the best available arrangement and certainly worth a trial. I hoped that her adjustment from a sheltered situation wouldn't be difficult and that she would continue to gain in ability as she had at St. Coletta's. The Special Ed classes could be a permanent solution for her.

To my dismay, the special classes I'd envisioned turned out to be one single class, made up of students of differing ages. Some were older, some younger than Lindsay. Some had greater ability. Some had less. I feared that the only class would be a mish-mash of too many ages and abilities in the same classroom. I needed to learn more about this special class before enrolling Lindsay. I received permission to observe it.

What an exciting eye-opener it was. These first teachers of Special Needs children deserved high praise. They understood the needs of their students and adapted activities and instruction to those needs. Teaching differing ages, differing levels of ability, differing individual quirks and challenges in the same classroom during limited school hours seemed an impossible task. Yet, those creative teachers achieved good results for many of their students.

On the appointed afternoon, I knocked on the classroom door and stepped over the threshold into a room filled with surprises. The first was a slip of a girl, about twelve with blonde curly hair, who hopped up from where she was seated, ran to me, hugged me and took my hand. She led me to the chair that the teacher placed for me. While doing so, the young hostess smiled happily, with every feature of her face. Plump pink cheeks, slightly slanting eyes, her happy disposition and eagerness to please, suggested she might be a child with Down syndrome. Kate was her name.

"Thank you for welcoming our guest, Kate. You've done a very nice job. Now, please go back to your seat," the twenty-something teacher said gently. Her dark, deep set eyes radiated kindness. Kate obeyed immediately.

The teacher, Gwen Anderson, greeted me. Tall, with brown hair cut short, dressed simply in a slim skirt and white blouse, she was the only other adult in the roomful of eighteen children. Each of those children had individual needs to be addressed. Miss Anderson had an air of competence. After she explained my presence to the class, she suggested that the students go back to their work. All went compliantly.

Another surprise was the youngsters' behavior. I know I didn't anticipate chaos, but the students were even quieter than I'd expected. Each was concentrating on what their group was doing, paying little attention to my distracting presence. Most were thoroughly engaged in small groups at tables around the room. For others, it was a book on a desk. As I walked between the tables, I learned that each small group might have a different project, depending on their interests and levels of ability.

Sun shining in the classroom's large windows, walls covered with pinned up student drawings of birds, flowers and snow scenes made the entire room cheerful. The class, itself, was a mixture. It included a few more boys than girls, whose ages appeared to range from twelve to the late teens, though it was hard to tell the exact age of several.

All were working. Some were studying. Some were putting together jigsaw puzzles that made words. Some were holding flash cards for each other. All, that is, except for one neatly dressed, sandy-haired boy in a far corner of the classroom. When I looked his way, he clapped his hands over his ears and put his head down on his desk. Then he began a repetitive twirling movement, bobbing up and down from his chair. He continued this behavior pattern while Miss Anderson was engaged with a group of four of the other students. She saw what the boy was doing, but she was hard-pressed to leave her group.

As soon as she was able to leave, without interrupting the other students, she left the group she was with. She picked up a large book from another table and unhurriedly approached the young man. Gently placing a hand on his shoulder to help him seat himself and stay seated, she asked him, "Jerry would you like to look at the pictures in this book?"

She opened it wide on the table in front of the boy, talked about the photographs in it and took his hand so they were turning pages together.

"That's very good," she said. "I'm proud of you. I'm sure you can do this by yourself." Jerry began to turn the pages fast, just glancing at the pictures. Mostly, he enjoyed the repetitive turning of the pages. Seeing him absorbed in what he was doing, Miss Anderson slowly left his side.

I recognized that Jerry could be autistic because of my contact with the children at St. Coletta's. In 1967, however, the diagnosis of autism as a spectrum of disorders, and even the word autism, was not part of common usage. Not until the 2000's did the impairments associated with autism and Aspberger's Syndrome become more commonly known. Sadly, it was because those impairments also became increasingly prevalent.

After half-an-hour I prepared to leave. With all of the children occupied, working on their various projects and contented, Miss Anderson took a few minutes to explain her successful methods.

"I divide the children into small groups where they can express their individual interests and work according to their abilities," she told me. "I consider their ages but that isn't the important criteria, their ability draws them to a certain group. They can move from one group to another as their skills improve or their interests change. If there are several at about the same level, I attempt to tailor a group to meet their individual skills.

"During the day, I'll work with one group until what they are doing catches their interest and they are fully occupied. Then I move on to the next," she said. "It works, because the children choose for themselves the group that most closely suits their ability and what they like to do." She continued, "If I bring the class something unusual they'll all gather, no matter what their level. Or if one child has a special problem or difficulty choosing a group, I can take some time to guide them. Generally, they progress in academic subjects at a rate comfortable for each individual."

"From day to day the number of children in each group may change." Describing some of what she brings to the class, she said, "Nights I put together whatever might intrigue the children. We've had guinea pigs in cages. We've planted flowers in pots. The children delight in caring for the flowers and watching how they thrive." As she listed several more of her offerings, I recalled the creative methods of another teacher I'd learned from. I was impressed by her methods of teaching subjects like arithmetic and with her dedication to her students. Certainly, extra special credit was due those first teachers of children with special needs. Not only were they devoted to their charges who were not easy to teach, but they were exceptionally creative in their innovative methods. I left the school that day, assured that this class would certainly be suitable for Lindsay. My impression of the class proved to be 100% correct. My impression of the school's suitability for Lindsay didn't deserve the same grade.

Lindsay's first two days went well. But by the third and fourth days I could tell that she was troubled.

"How did it go today?" I asked after school that Thursday.

"O.K."

"How do you like the school?"

"O.K." She was less than enthusiastic. Her tone said that something was bothering her.

"What's wrong?" I asked her. It took a few more questions for her to find the right words. "They teased me," she said.

"How did they tease you?"

"They called me *retard.*"

"In your class?" I was puzzled. Lindsay's description came as a surprise. During my visit to the class I'd seen no signs of prejudice and hadn't expected any. I quickly learned that the problem wasn't with the class

"The lunch room," she told me, "After school. I didn't like it."

I'd hoped that the changes in attitudes toward *special* children meant that the other students would gradually accept them. But it was too soon to expect those long term built-in attitudes to change. This problem for Lindsay required a different solution.

Though the nuns St. Coletta's could be strict, the students were treated with respect and kindness. Lindsay was encouraged to excel at the level of her ability. She was not disdained because she was *different*. Grouped with youngsters of similar ages and capabilities she blossomed. Lindsay fit in comfortably with her peers. Her protected years at St. Coletta's didn't prepare her for cruel behavior by schoolmates she didn't know. In the local Middle School, Special Ed students were ridiculed by other students. During lunch hour, and after school, when they were mingled with the other children the word "*retard*" was flung at them and it stung.

"What is *retard*?" Lindsay asked me with tears in her eyes. I was at an immediate loss to try to explain the situation. I had to think about words that wouldn't be hurtful or decrease her self-confidence.

"I'll tell you later," I procrastinated and changed the subject. *How does one explain inconsiderate rudeness to the person who might be hurt?* After I'd given an answer to her question a lot of thought and hoped I'd found the right words to ease her unhappiness, we talked.

"Sometimes children, who haven't been taught to be considerate, call other children names they think are funny or smart," I told Lindsay.

"Sometimes they don't know what the word means, they've just heard it. *Retard* is a word like that. What *retard* really means is "to make something slow down." I accented the second syllable rather than the first.

I said, "Kids believe that someone in Special Ed class thinks more slowly than they do. But they don't really know the person they're talking about. They don't consider all of the good qualities that person might have, even if they do think more slowly. For example, you have so many good qualities."

"Good qualities?" Lindsay asked me.

"Of course you do. You're nice to people. You're fun to be with. Let's give everyone a little time to know you better. We'll hope that they stop teasing you. If they were older, they would understand more about you and not tease. They wouldn't tease anyone else, either."

Sadly, for Lindsay, time was no solution. Although I spoke with the teacher and principal, they couldn't control what students did when they weren't around. The teasing continued. Used to being protected for six years, Lindsay became deeply hurt. She couldn't put her pain into words or stand up for herself. She simply wanted to stop going to that school.

I began to search for a better solution. With training in social work, knowing what to look for, where to find it and how to persevere until successful, I felt confident that I would find the specialized resources and services to suit my daughter's needs.

Meanwhile, Lindsay bravely remained at school. For two months I searched for a better situation, using all resources available to me at the time. But too often, when I believed I'd found the right answer, further delving dissuaded me. One special school was too far distant. Another boarding facility was too expensive. For tutoring, transportation was a problem. The only solution available was having a sitter stay with Lindsay while I worked.

Fortunately, summer vacation arrived at about the time I realized there was no satisfactory alternative to the Middle School. It helped that for three months Lindsay could stay away from it. A neighbor's high-school age daughter, Mary Lee, stayed with Lindsay during the days. This successful arrangement evolved into a saving grace for my daughter in many ways.

"I'm a Girl Scout"

Mary Lee came to our house more often than when she was paid to be with Lindsay. She truly enjoyed being with my daughter. One morning she stopped by to invite Lindsay to her Girl Scout troop meeting that afternoon. Thrilled at the thought, Lindsay found it hard to wait until the appointed hour. She was still bubbling with excitement and couldn't be still after the meeting while Mary Lee told me that Lindsay was invited to join their troop.

From the beginning, Lindsay felt welcomed by the girls in the Scout troop. She flourished, bringing home cupcakes she baked, cards and pictures she'd drawn and flower arrangements the Scouts helped her make. I was eager to watch how Lindsay fit in with girls so far above her intellectual level and suggested the troop meet one day at our house. Having been a Scout myself and a leader when Cary's turn came, I was familiar with the organization.

During the meeting in our home, I quietly observed the kindness with which Lindsay was included. Mary Lee's actions set an example for the Scouts who were still learning how to work with Lindsay. That day's project was a step toward earning their first aid badge. They assembled first aid kits and rolled and applied bandages. Interesting to me was watching how each of the girls wanted to be the one to help Lindsay. Still, some sensed exactly how to do so while others were uncomfortable, though well-meaning.

This was one of the times I learned the importance of paving the way for those who've never associated with a child who had special needs. Many don't know what to expect. Many are uneasy interacting with someone different. I learned to explain my daughter, beginning with the words, "In many ways Lindsay isn't like other people but in many ways she is. The way Lindsay is different, is that she can't learn as quickly as others learn. It takes her longer to catch up and there are some things she can't do. But if you are patient with her, she will try her best.

"In many ways Lindsay is the same as you. She has the same feelings you do. She can be just as happy or sad. She wants to be your friend. You can approach her and talk with her just as with anyone else. But don't be dismayed by times when her reactions aren't what you expect."

In so many instances those words were enough. As Lindsay grew older, I discovered it was equally important to prepare adults for what to expect with my daughter. They become more comfortable when they can laugh with us about funny things she does. When people begin to know Lindsay they find her to be fun, funny and genuinely interesting.

The day of the meeting, it was easy to recognize the most understanding and compassionate Scout, the one most at ease with Lindsay. A girl named Beth stood out. A bit pudgy with dimples, neat in her uniform and wearing a smile that could melt an iceberg, Beth took Lindsay to the corner of a table where other girls were working. She painstakingly chose one item of the project materials at a time, explained it and laid it in front of Lindsay. She showed Lindsay what each was used for and had her place them one by one in the first aid kit. Each girl applied a band aid to her partner. After Beth showed her how, Lindsay managed perfectly. So it went, until Lindsay was ecstatic—as an eight-year-old would be ecstatic—with the First Aid kit she assembled *all by herself.*

"Will I Be on Television?"

Lindsay remained unaware that she was not treated as the other girls' equal. The Scouts were learning to be kind to someone less fortunate and it took a while for them to see her as a real person. In the beginning they thought of Lindsay as their project but little by little their perspective changed. They began to learn from Lindsay as she learned from them.

In the Scouts' eyes Lindsay gradually became one of them. Her hard work to earn a merit badge and her efforts to keep up were infectious. Each Scout vied to be the one to help her. The girls encouraged her quips and giggles that made their projects more fun.

Lindsay responded with the same kindness the Scouts offered her. The troop members slowly realized her value as a person. They treated her as their friend, inviting her to join them at the ice cream parlor, on shopping trips for the troop's craft materials and to attend slumber parties. Her ability to show her worth as a person, against enormous odds, earned her their respect and admiration.

Membership in the Girl Scout troop marked a new step upward in Lindsay's growing self-confidence. While her intelligence remained at the level of an eight-year-old, her emotional reactions of delight and fun made her a joy to be with.

Being a Girl Scout not only helped Lindsay, years later it helped other girls with special needs.. Dorothy, one of the Scouts, was a member the High School class of 1973. She used her scouting experience to become an adult troop leader in her town in central New Jersey.

When we talked about her high school years, Dorothy began by telling me how their two troop leaders prepared the Scouts for Lindsay's joining the troop. "We were coached about Lindsay's abilities. We learned what to say." Honest in her approach, she continued, "Learning how to work with the developmentally disabled doesn't come naturally. Having Lindsay in the troop, we all learned something. We learned how to accept, how to include, how to be courteous. We were prepped to be ready to accept the challenge to include Lindsay in the troop."

Now, as a Girl Scout leader herself, Dorothy has had as many as five developmentally disabled girls in the troop at the same time. She said, "We all benefitted because of the experience with Lindsay. "We would have many more, but the number is limited because of the extra attention those girls require. Once you've had that experience it opens your eyes."

Years later I also had the privilege of observing a pre-school class that instituted "mingling." Developmentally disabled pre-school children were mingled with an average group of other preschool children. It is a new method of making these children accepted members of society. I was told that if other children are with the disavantaged youngsters prior to kindergarten, they are more comfortable and never consider them as different. They know they are different, but they are more patient and kind.

It is similar to what Lindsay experienced with the Girl Scouts. I was told that the same thing I saw with the Girl Scouts was true in the pre-school. The other children vie to be the ones to help those they sense as needy.

As the months went by the Scouts remained innocently normal young girls, while the world was changing drastically around them. For Cary, in college, the hippie movement and Vietnam protests became a reality. At her college, a man named Tommy the Traveler worked at inciting the students to protest violently, convincing them to bomb the ROTC office located in the basement of a dormitory. One of Cary's friends was "busted" for drug use and another acquaintance nearly went to prison for growing marijuana at home. We parents feared that our children could be caught in the 'counter culture.'

Cary phoned from college one night and startled me by asking, "May I go to Washington to march on the Capitol?"

Surprised, I asked, "Why do you want to go?"

"Because everybody's going." It didn't take more than a half-second for me to answer, "No, you can't go."

"O.K," she said. That was that. I'm sure my sigh of relief could be heard long distance.

Another call was the Woodstock phone call. "May I go to Woodstock?" Crowds of young people from all over the country were planning to gather at a farm in New York for a weekend of music. Again, my answer was "no." Again, Cary accepted my answer. It was a good thing since it became a weekend of sex, drugs and rock and roll.

When parents of teenagers were together in groups, our talk was serious. We worried about new influences and protests that could adversely affect our children. Newspapers reported that radical organizations were spreading across the land, launching protests to achieve political goals. We heard their names; Black Panthers, Students for a Democratic Society (SDS), the Weathermen…many of whom believed in violence and acts of terrorism. Young revolutionaries participated in "sit ins" and bombings in New York in the early 70s. Some died. We were terrified that our children would believe slogans such as "Don't trust anyone over 30," and "Kill your parents."

To this day, I believe that it was our family's challenges that kept my children from making mistakes that might have destroyed their futures. Misplaced trust and flawed judgment destroyed too many young people during those years. I was grateful for our team of four, solid in togetherness as we surmounted difficult problems. Lindsay, in her way, added her share to the team by pitching in.

Our home nestled in the foothills of the Pocono Mountains. On a clear day, from our perch near the top of one of the higher hills we could see Manhattan's skyline. At the crest of the hill a few doors from us, the large Colonial style home of the Truscott family overflowed with six children. Their second child, Betsy, was similar to Lindsay in that she, too, was mentally challenged. Though Betsy's mother, Sue, was considerably older than I was, we became close friends. Sue's garden, overlooking a wooded valley below, was a sea of dreams. In spring we lounged in large rattan chairs under white blooms of dogwood.

Through the summer our friendship deepened and we shared personal problems. Though it was hard for Sue to talk about, a new son-in-law was making no secret of his avoidance of Betsy. Sue's story came out in bits and pieces as each new cruelty by the new family member resulted in Sue's increasing depth of anguish and sadness.

At the Prescott's engagement party for the two of them, friends warned Sue to be wary of the young man's mother. "There's something wrong," several told Sue. "But it was too late to do anything about it," Sue said. "My daughter was in love and I believed I shouldn't interfere. Now, I wish I'd done so."

Sue talked about his "lies to avoid being with us. It's hard for our daughter who loves family celebrations. She's no longer permitted to share our family holidays."

Sue talked about Betsy's recent birthday party. "Betsy knows she's being avoided. Too often her feelings are hurt by what she doesn't understand. She asks if she's done something wrong and I have to assure her that she has not made any mistakes."

More and more Betsy came to our house to play with Lindsay while Sue and I spent at least one afternoon a week together. Sue came to our home with Betsy, or Lindsay and I went to Sue's. We became even closer friends, attempting to replace Sue's concern and frustration with our two special needs daughters' small successes. Betsy played the guitar and helped Lindsay learn to strum. The girls created their own idea of a school with Lindsay's flash cards and books they pretended to read. One Thanksgiving Day Betsy serenaded our entire family with the music of her guitar.

Sue heard of another family facing the similar behavior of a new member. We mused about possible solutions and decided that the best would be counseling with a trained, objective advisor. I was quietly grateful for the closeness and loyalty of my three children and the security of my belief that nothing like this could happen to our family.

For almost a month while the Scout troop took a vacation, Sue's and my visits were postponed while the children and I traveled.

The first leg of our trip was to my parents' home in the Midwest. Bruce remained with them while Cary, Lindsay and I flew to California. Since Lindsay was used to air travel and had gained self-confidence as a Girl Scout, I had no concerns about her joining Cary and me. My mistake was not allowing for the full impact of her newly discovered self-confidence. We learned, to our dismay, that Lindsay's new confidence encouraged her to take on an entire airline. Her luggage did not arrive on the carousel at Baggage Claim.

The past Christmas her gift wish was for "two new luggages." The Grasshopper brand of distinctively patterned suitcases was all the rage… particularly for young girls. Her heart was set on it. She was beyond delight opening her gifts and discovering her wish had been granted.

The luggage problem arose when we departed the plane in San Francisco. A fellow passenger, having the same patterned suitcases, mistakenly claimed Lindsay's. Not only were her suitcases missing from the carousel, they were not found in the airline's baggage office. Lindsay was furious.

We were urged to check into our hotel and promised that the missing luggage would be delivered as soon as it was located. Those promises meant nothing to my daughter. She wouldn't budge from the airline office until her adored suitcases were returned. Cary and I explained. We cajoled. We were embarrassed. When we finally got her to a cab we almost lifted her in.

That was only the beginning. Lindsay was not only furious at the airline, her fury targeted Cary and me when we attempted to explain and calm her. She refused to come into the hotel room and sat outside the door — on the floor—in the hall, awaiting delivery. Fortunately, her luggage arrived not long afterward and peace reigned once again. Soon, we were having a fine time in San Francisco.

I was eager to show the girls the beauty of the Nine Mile Drive out of San Francisco. We took the drive south and it was as beautiful as I remembered. From it, the approach to the West Coast Highway was smooth and easy. We couldn't have asked for a more beautiful and sunny day.

A sheer drop below, on the passenger side of the car, the Pacific Ocean was cobalt blue with a high pounding surf. On the driver's side of the road, walls of mountain were almost near enough to touch. The road was made for beautiful and carefree driving. Cary sat on the back seat with Lindsay, creating detailed word pictures of the magnificence of the scenery. I can't recall at what point I began to wonder about the lack of other traffic. We seemed alone on the road for miles.

What I can recall is that our drive from San Francisco to Los Angeles was even more hair-raising than the lost luggage episode. My questioning of the empty highway was answered by a terrifying deep crack in the roadbed, tapering out to becoming wider and bottomless on the ocean side. I saw the crack just in time. Just in time, I saw slightly more than a car-width space between the solid rock wall on my left and the narrow part of the crack. I saw it just in time to turn enough, not quite scraping the wall and feeling only a bump as we drove safely over the crack.

Fortunately, neither girl was aware of our potential catastrophe. After leaving the highway at the next possible exit, I was told "the Pacific Coast Highway was closed because of dangerous breaks in the roadway. There was a notice in the newspaper." We never saw a sign or a barrier of any kind.

We also had a fine time in Los Angeles. That was until we arrived at the airport for the flight home and discovered that Lindsay had not fully recovered from her outrage at the airline. At the check-in line she barged her way to the front of the line, ignoring everyone else ahead of her. With the fury we'd seen in San Francisco, she announced to the woman at the ticket desk, "I don't want you to lose my luggage this time!"

With the same angry tone of voice, she said, "You lost it once. The second time I don't know where you hid it. But you better not lose it this time." The poor startled attendant had no idea how to react.

One of us, either Cary or I nabbed Lindsay and brought her back into the ticket line. Lindsay's words must have made an impression. After that flight her two suitcases were the second pieces out on the baggage carousel.

When we arrived home, we learned that Sue's problem had a happy ending. While we were away she spent time with a counselor. She said that her son-in-law agreed to counseling and recognized what he was missing. "He learned how much their future children would be missing by not being part of a loving family, especially not being able to enjoy the love of grandparents." Sue said, "They plan to have children." She told me that her son-in-law was making a genuine effort and she could see that her daughter was so much happier in her marriage. "Betsy is pleased when we're all together."

"I Want to Make My Own Decisions"

Cary was proving to be a success at everything she attempted. Bruce and I were as close as two-peas-in-a-pod, working together to surmount each hurdle as it came our way. Young as he was, he was the man of the family. Cary and Bruce, their friends, and the Girl Scouts of the troop included Lindsay and helped her. With her little girl reactions, she was funny and fun.

I was proud of my three children. I basked in the strength of our small family and was certain nothing could ever part the four of us. Even our stalwart collie dog contributed her share of serendipity, producing five puppies that looked like cuddly teddy bears. Above all, we'd kept our sense of humor through the most difficult of times; times that played a large part in developing the lasting family mantra, *if you don't know whether to laugh or cry, laugh!*

Beginning in 1965 attitudes toward the mentally disabled began to change. Anne Burke, an Illinois Supreme Court Justice, wrote, "[The children] were either in a state institution or in a closet."

Justice Burke initiated programs for mentally disabled children. In 1968, with Eunice Kennedy Shriver, she founded the Special Olympics, a sporting competition for children with intellectual disabilities. Aided by the support of Shriver and Kennedy families and volunteers, public and financial backing for the Special Olympics increased. As the competition grew internationally and drew increasing attention, changing attitudes, changing vocabulary and the publicized special events led to a lessening of prejudice.

Most easily recognized were the smiling faces of those openly identified as having the developmental disability identified as Down syndrome. Not only were they no longer being hidden away, they were successful at what they attempted and they were being valued as individuals of worth. As these children and adults became a more familiar part of the community, those with other mental disabilities were increasingly accepted and respected. There were a few schools that provided a setting where children with developmental disabilities were valued and fostered, but they were small and not well known. In addition to St. Coletta's school there was another in Kentucky. The Stewart Home School, founded in Frankfort, Kentucky in 1893 was a forerunner dedicated to the education and enrichment of students with intellectual disabilities. But as the Special Olympics became publicly-supported events, acceptance of intellectual disabilities followed. In Illinois and Kansas City new schools were founded to educate the developmentally disabled.

———◆•❙◆❙•◆———

As the world of the disabled was changing for the better, the same was happening in our lives. The culmination of events surrounding the crash took place during a week-long jury trial. Bruce and I re-lived the trauma and its aftermath with our testimony. We found the jury to be attentive and sympathetic, having a sense of humor, when Bruce at eight-years, obviously all boy, was asked about his fractured shoulder, "Do you have any pain left?"

"Only, when I play my violin?" He brought down the house.

The jury unanimously found that the driver who illegally careened from behind a slow-moving farm vehicle, head-on into my car in our lane, was 100% guilty. Not only did insurance relieve our financial problems, the funds helped Cary complete her schooling to graduation and saw Bruce through four years of university education.

During Cary's third year in college, she introduced us to a fellow Lacrosse player she'd met in college. Of medium height, powerful build, with hair the color of a sandy beach, Bill fit the ideal picture of an athlete. He also was smart. Bill lived in a nearby town and during the ensuing summer vacation, this gentle giant spent considerable time in our home. With Bill's psychology training he was drawn to Lindsay. He was intrigued by her ability to learn despite her disability. He became devoted to her and they spent long hours together. His patience instructing her was remarkable. His thoughtfulness of her special needs was compelling.

Bill taught her to knit. Because of her knitting accomplishments, during breaks he taught her to pluck the strings of his guitar. She glowed when we clapped our encouragement of her strumming. Our pleasure showed, too, when we admired her learning and performing for the rest of us. In his very individual way, Bill knitted himself into the life of our family.

These were also the years that the word "baggage" took on new meaning in the lives of divorced men and women. "Baggage" became the simile for obligations and responsibilities that one, or both, partners would bring to a second marriage. In many cases it meant the children. Should a second marriage be contemplated by two adults in love, the developmental disability of one child might be insurmountable "baggage," preventing a permanent relationship. I believed that to be true, so remarriage never entered my mind. Concentrating on my children, my advancing career and continuing recuperation, I gave a second marriage no thought. Only one time, did a classmate of Cary's arrange a date for me with her father, who also had been through a divorce. The evening was a total flop for both of us.

But I didn't count on Betty, my dearest friend in Minneapolis, stirring a magic pot. On a trip back to visit her, Betty introduced me to her brother, Buddy. He became the force behind the happiest years of my life and those of my children. To him, the word "baggage" simply meant the suitcases one carried on trips. We married. My family, "baggage" and all, moved back to Minneapolis.

Returning to Minneapolis was like coming home again to the allure and exhilaration of crisp seasons, glistening lakes and the warmth of arms around my shoulders. I'd become a member of the family I loved. I had the joy of renewing long-time friendships.

As we searched for a school for Lindsay, we soon discovered that Minnesota's Governor, Hubert Humphrey, who had his own family member with special needs, focused his and his wife's attention on state benefits for mentally disadvantaged youngsters. This included education, housing and financial aid. Particularly, it included a school for children with special needs in a suburb of Minneapolis. The school, named Glen Lake School, enrolled children in special classes up to the age of twenty-one. Only a small tuition was charged to cover books and class extras. The highly recommended public school offered classes and activities, suited to the needs of the intellectually challenged, and were taught by teachers who were college-trained in Special Education. Day students could live at home and attend classes. Lindsay's continuing education problems appeared to be solved.

Only Lindsay didn't see the situation in quite the same light as the rest of us. Her teenage rebellion burst forth just when it was most important for her to behave. At a most inauspicious time she decided to assert herself.

On the day of her enrollment interview, my four-foot-eight-inch teenager appeared in a red plaid skirt that clashed unmerci-

"Will I Be on Television?"

fully with a hippy tie-dyed orange and black tee shirt. She wore her dirtiest tennis shoes and a misshapen cardigan.

"You can't go to the interview dressed like that," I said.

"Yes, I can."

"No, you can't. Come with me. You're going to change."

"No, I won't," she glared. "I want to make my own dishishons," she told me in a tone of voice not unlike stamping her foot. Was this my compliant daughter who rarely questioned what I asked her to do? Though she finally changed to the outfit I selected, we paid for her concession at the interview. Repeatedly, she interrupted the admissions counselor. She hopped up from her chair and tried to climb on my lap. She wandered around the office pulling books from the bookshelves. Her behavior was new to me. Never before had I witnessed anything like it. We were summarily but tactfully dismissed with the words, "we'll call you when we determine the class that will best suit Lindsay."

Was it possible that my daughter's treatment as an equal in the scout troop made her think she no longer had special needs? Was she convinced that special needs education was beneath her level? Was she letting me know, in her own way, that she didn't want to attend Glen Lake School? Was it because she felt she belonged with typical students in the public schools?

The admission counselor may have wondered, too, for no one from the school called us back. Quite the contrary, I called the school to plead Lindsay's case. Fortunately, I spoke to the Special Education counselor who was well-trained. She understood when I explained my reasoning about my daughter's actions and told her, "Lindsay is usually well-mannered."

"Let's give it a try," she offered.

At Glen Lake school, my daughter adjusted quickly and made new friends. She discovered that she loved the school, and her reading improved amazingly, quite enough for her to astound me one night.

Lindsay's concentrated quick-flipping of the pages of magazines, more or less pretending to read, was nothing new. I believed that she only looked at the pictures until the night she held a magazine open in her lap and said, "Can I vote when I'm twenty-one?" I couldn't believe she'd read what I'd heard her say until I saw the magazine's page. Lindsay read aloud, "21? Be sure to vote." I hoped my astonishment in her increasing ability didn't show, as we talked about what it meant to be of voting age and to understand the privilege.

Among Lindsay's 'friends at Glen Lake School were children with Down syndrome and other intellectual disabilities. The young boys could think of nothing else but their coming athletic games. They bounced instead of walking in the school halls. They threw volley balls at each other on the playground. They could barely sit still in the classroom as the day of the event approached. They were practicing to participate in the Special Olympics, the sports competitions founded by Justice Burke and Eunice Kennedy Shriver in 1965. For these youngsters the Special Olympics were whopping in their impact.

Local parents slowly drew in community leaders. Local newspapers gave the games coverage. The children were admired rather than shunned.

One outstanding example of local promotion is Race for the Champions, founded by the Sallaroulo family of South Florida to honor their son, Patrick, a young man with Down syndrome. The race was founded on the belief that "everyone deserves a chance, an opportunity to live a fulfilled life." The 5K walk includes the best athletes in the area walking with others who have mental and physical disabilities. The numbers of those involved, including community and corporate leaders, add up to 1,500 to 2,000 participants a year.

A resulting landmark decision was to move Special Olympics headquarters to the Nova University campus where the disabled youth will have the opportunity to interact with college students and the

"Will I Be on Television?"

students will have the opportunity to know the athletes as the courageous individuals they are.

Lindsay's class also included teenagers with autism. In 1998, Dustin Hoffman's outstanding portrayal of a savant with autism improved public awareness. Its message was to accommodate autistic people and make use of the abilities they have.

The word "autism," from the Greek word "autos" meaning self, has been in use for 100 years. It describes conditions in which a person is removed from social interaction, thus, an isolated self. From the early 1900's it has referred to one of the symptoms of schizophrenia.

For Lindsay, the years at Glen Lake School rank high on her scale of happiness. It would have been her wish to continue indefinitely at Glen Lake, only her twenty-first year loomed. Age twenty-one was the cut-off age for government benefits offered to the disabled. Since that time the law was changed in some states to require schooling to be offered until the twenty-second birthday.

Glen Lake School was one of the "twenty-one-age" states. Under ordinary circumstances, when your child becomes twenty-one, he or she is an adult and you offer your blessings and send them off to fly on their own wings. Under ordinary circumstances, it's a time for you to relax, knowing you've done your best to prepare them. The rest is up to them.

When Lindsay became twenty-one she wasn't prepared to fly on her own. I was faced with a question that had no answer for parents like me. "What is available for my developmentally disabled child after age twenty-one?"

Looking back and writing about Lindsay's earlier years, I make them sound almost easy; a crisis solved, a challenge conquered, a hurdle jumped. They weren't easy. Life isn't easy when emotions are like a roller coaster. Still, the light at the end of the tunnel is the joy these special children bring. We understand the challenges they face. We're touched by their gallantry and their effort to carve out their special place in the world. They offer us indescribable admiration, happiness and love.

In return, at that time, we knew of nothing we could offer Lindsay that would contribute the slightest measure of satisfaction for her future.

"We Learned to Love our New Family"

Nothing was available for Lindsay. She was as bored as a caged lion, at home each day with time on her hands. Her twenty-first birthday had come and gone. No longer was she eligible for public school or government sponsored activity. For her, days at home with only repetitious TV and my company soon reached the ultimate of uninteresting. "How about learning to cook?" I asked.

"Mother," she said, "I can't do that, you know that I'm brain damaged." When I stopped laughing I had to admit she was creative with excuses.

We tried movies, picnic lunches in parks. Museums were too complicated for her to appreciate. In public, she encountered the same problem the special needs youngsters of Glen Lake School met during school field trips, "People make fun of us." This reaction hurt. You could see it in her eyes, though she neither acknowledged nor talked about it. Activities like the Special Olympics called attention to the likability and courage of these children but stigma wasn't easily erased.

The more I researched the more I discovered that for Lindsay no ongoing stimulating or productive activity was available. Her twenty-first birthday marked an unwelcome road block, replacing happy times at Glen Lake school. She desperately missed her school and her schoolmates.

Though twenty-one, Lindsay was still a teenager in her development. She'd gone through each stage of growth, baby, toddler, child, puberty, only she had been through each stage at a later age than the average child. At twenty-one her actions and reactions were those of a teenager. She wasn't prepared for the years ahead as an adult might have been.

Just at the time I was most discouraged, we received a surprise phone call from a stranger. The man, who described himself as the director of a local private school for the mentally disabled, asked if he could pay Buddy and me a visit. He seemed pleasant on the phone and after more detailed conversation, I agreed.

Four nights later, Jerry Gross, an eager thirty-something redhead in a blazer jacket and tie, appeared at our front door. Looking as if he'd be far more comfortable in sports clothes than what he wore, he carried a large sheaf of architectural drawings under his arm. He lost no time in laying out the plans on our dining table. He introduced what he wanted to show us, and said, "Parents of young people like Lindsay have overriding concerns. One is, "How can my child remain active and productive while growing older?"

He understood exactly what we were experiencing with Lindsay and talked about it in some detail. "The second overriding concern," he said, "Is what will happen to my child when I'm no longer around?" He described the planning stages of a new project offering lifetime care and ongoing activity.

In the East, I'd attended two meetings of small groups of parents attempting to creatively solve the problems Jerry Gross talked about. One meeting accomplished little and never reconvened. The other group's ideas were met with a collective yawn. So, my immediate reaction to Jerry Gross' project was quiet cynicism.

"Three men and I purchased farm land from the mayor of the small town of Victoria, west of Minneapolis," Jerry Gross told us. "We plan to build three low rise units, around a nicely landscaped central courtyard, each housing twelve residents." On the plan he

"Will I Be on Television?"

traced the projecting wings of one of the buildings. "Each wing will have three bedrooms and a large bathroom. Men will be in one wing, women in the other. The common co-ed facilities are living room, dining room and kitchen."

By the end of the evening Buddy and I knew a great deal about what would become one of the earliest communities of group homes for the developmentally disabled in the United States. My doubts about the project began to recede.

The next steps for the men, one of whom was the mayor of the town, were a series of meetings seeking agreement from the community's residents to establish the group homes in their neighborhood.

An early staff member tells the story, "We brought a group of several potential residents into a Mr. Donut shop in the town and the entire restaurant emptied. Just when we thought every thing would move smoothly, we faced a big reality check," she said.

"We faced *nimby*," Jerry Gross reminisced years later. "The general consensus was *'your idea is a fine way to help the developmentally disabled, but not in my backyard.'* Thereafter, the men worked diligently to promote a greater understanding among the townsfolk.

"For quite a while we were rowing upstream," Jerry Gross said. "Built-in prejudice was difficult to combat. We succeeded because of the mayor. He was a respected and favorite member of the community. Those who would be the immediate neighbors eventually understood. Fortunately, their compassion took precedence over their fears."

Years later, and retired, Jerry Gross wrote me, "We wanted to offer developmentally disabled adults a home and a normal way of life." He added, "Small family setting. Utilizing community sources.

"As long as we could meet their needs, they could call Community Living home and stay the rest of their lives.

"We were blessed with forty-three years of living out a dream."

Lindsay was Community Living's second resident. Sometime later, when I talked about the history of the homes with Angie, that early dedicated staff member still at CLI, she said to me, "You had an easier choice, to put Lindsay in an institution and forget her. But you didn't do it." She added, "Soon, we had a waiting list. People in state institutions that had been warehoused lined up to move in."

It was interesting to watch the town's attitude change as locals began to know the Community Living residents as individuals. Welcomed by name in local restaurants, Lindsay is offered her choice of table or booth and members of the restaurant's staff pause in what they're doing to greet her with a cheery, "Hello, glad to see you, Lindsay."

Community Living was incorporated in 1970 and adopted the acronym CLI. The dedication featured Minnesota Governor Humphrey's wife, Muriel, and Father Val, the local priest whose homily included the words, "Sometimes God gives us a crooked line in order to make it straight."

Similar construction of Intermediate Care Facilities for the Developmentally Disabled (ICF-DD) followed this initial example in other parts of the country. Some were government funded, some private. Though in 2013 there still are not enough to meet the important need, single facilities and communities of group homes can be located by searching, either via the Internet or state by state.

About the time we were involved in the birth of CLI, Cary's friend Bill, the knitter, was slowly knitting his way into the midst of our family. He became our son-in-law. Bill and Cary ventured from the East to Minneapolis and because of his experience with

"Will I Be on Television?"

Lindsay and his Psychology degree, we suggested that Bill talk to those directing CLI. The result proved better than we could have imagined. Bill's interview launched mutual interest. Though no opening for him was immediately available, a position was open for a house parent. If Cary, with her background in education, applied and was accepted, Bill could live with her in one of the homes as an unpaid volunteer.

"Two weeks later, hardly back from our honeymoon," Cary said, "We had twelve children."

Each home, called Cottage 1, 2, or 3, was home to six men and six women, each resident had differing and demanding needs. The very first night, Tom, one of the men who took great pride in his appearance, brushed his teeth with Ben-Gay, the aching joint ointment.

Cary recalls, "Within the next two weeks, I was cooking and doing laundry for fourteen people." She and Bill still talk and laugh about their first years of married life. Cary planned menus, shopped for groceries, spent activity time with their charges and taught them. Bill, in title, did maintenance work. But in reality, he performed all the duties of a caring house parent.

"As strange as it may seem, we learned to love our new family," they say as they tell the stories. "Each member of our 'family' had an individual personality. We treasured them for their idiosyncrasies. Alvin, who only spoke unintelligible German, would come out in his adored stretchy royal blue pajamas to go to work. He didn't want to take them off and sometimes he put his pants on over them."

"Big John, at sixty years, tall, thin, wearing sweaters and glasses and looking like a retired professor, prided himself on being a real gentleman. He'd take his morning 'Constitutional,' walking to the lumber yard and the post office, ending at the coffee shop where he'd have his morning cup of coffee. He greeted people when he saw them. Those who didn't know him thought he was the Mayor. They loved him."

One morning Bill had to sideline him from his Constitutional because of his behavior. Not to be sidelined, he climbed out the window to go downtown.

Cary's concern for their charges is obvious as she reminisces. "Bob was very quiet and nice. He managed his wheelchair by himself. He was a happy and friendly man.

"Albert, who couldn't talk, also had Down syndrome. In his 50's he'd raise his hand to say 'Hi.' It was all he could say. Albert had to have his large toy semi-trailer truck at his feet at all times and sat for hours with his truck in the living room."

As the Special Olympics became well known, athletes with Down syndrome became widely applauded for their courage and success. Nevertheless, because of distinguishing facial features, attitudes about Down syndrome were tied to racism and colonialism until as recently as the 1970s. In the 20th century, Down syndrome and its identifiable facial features had become the most recognizable form of developmental disability.

Until the middle of the 20th century, the cause of Down syndrome remained unknown. Standard medical texts assumed it was caused by a combination of inheritable factors which had not been identified. Other theories focused on injuries sustained at birth.

In 1959 Professor Langdon Down discovered that the condition resulted from an extra chromosome, subsequently labeled as the 21st, and the condition as trisomy 21. In 1961, geneticists, and in 1965 those in the World Health Organization, officially adopted the name Down syndrome for the condition.

Cary continued her description of the residents in the cottage, "Cathy, in her late twenties, with a mind of her own, loved her shoes. The only way to have her cooperate was to take her shoes."

Cary's years as a house mother include the night she planned to have liver for dinner. "Liver wasn't anyone's favorite but I thought I'd flavored it enough with tomato soup to disguise it.

"Will I Be on Television?"

I thought the residents might enjoy it. "I didn't want to take any chances by putting liver on the written menu, so I wrote Beef and Gravy and didn't say another word about dinner in advance. "Donna was our carrot-top, a red head, short, chubby, always sporting a huge smile, always jolly and exuberant. Donna sat down at the table. She took one look. She stood up in a flash and shouted THIS IS LIVER!"

"That," said Cary, "ended dinner for everyone."

In age the residents were from their late teens to their sixties. As Bill reminisces, he smiles, "Before we began, I had a plan in mind, of organization and scheduling. Bill said, "By the second day that plan went out the window. Each of our charges had their individual behavior plan. If we'd tried a stringent scheduling plan, it would have been like herding cats."

He recalls, "As soon as we began to understand their different needs, their individual schedules fell into place. Our working with them fell into place, too."

One of Bill's examples was David, a handsome dark-haired man in his thirties who was extremely withdrawn. He feared social contact and avoided it as much as was possible in a group home. His entire conversation was marked by a constant repetition of the words "every day." David would sit, hardly moving in his favorite living room chair day after day, starting every one of the stories he told, "every day and every day and every day." On occasion David would exhibit short bursts of anger that Bill was always able to calm.

David's symptoms, an inability to easily communicate and interact with others, were among those recognized as autistic.

In 1943, Leo Kanner, a German immigrant psychiatrist at Johns Hopkins University, first clearly delineated and described autism. He used the term "autism" to describe the lack of social interaction. In 1944, Hans Asperger, who worked in Germany during World War II in isolation from scientists in the US, described a similar condition. He focused on cases of those with normal IQs. Many of Kanner's patients also had normal IQs, but he included the entire range of language and intelligence. His diagnostic criteria, still in use today, were (1) abnormal development of social interaction and (2) repetitive behavior and the "obsessive desire for the maintenance of sameness."

The general public was largely uninformed about autism at the time Bill and Cary were house parents at CLI. The first time many heard the word autistic was in the 1988 movie Rain Man, starring a young Tom Cruise and Dustin Hoffman. Mr. Hoffman was made famous by his portrayal of Raymond, an autistic man who had a remarkable rote memory. He could always win playing Black Jack.

Lucy was one of the older residents in the Cottage. With no previous warning of poor physical health, one night Lucy had an unexpected stroke. While Cary remained in the Cottage to care for the others, Bill went with her to the hospital. He sat by her bedside for three days. He left the hospital only for brief periods of sleep and returned to be there for her as quickly as possible. Bill's devotion to the clients who depended on him convinced the owners of CLI that he had the compassion necessary to become the director of CLI, a position he held until retirement thirty-three years later.

In 2013 Community Living, Incorporated, was purchased from the original owner-developers by Bethesda Lutheran Communities of Wisconsin. Nothing was changed in the CLI organization, not the facility, the residents or staff members. All remained the same as before the sale and purchase.

"I'm Employee of the Month"

"*Work*" was one of the words that snagged my thoughts during Jerry Gross' presentation to us. All public education would cease for Lindsay on her twenty-first birthday. The possibility of a job remained in my mind throughout the building of CLI and during her move into Cottage Two. If she could be employed, her life would be filled with purpose and activity.

Shortly after her arrival at CLI, I learned that while the wider world of employment wasn't available for those with special needs, a remarkable facility I'd completely forgotten had been slowly and successfully taking shape. The truth of the saying, "*Mighty Oaks from little Acorns grow,*" perfectly fit that facility. It was named Opportunity Workshop.

Turning back the pages of my memory to sixteen years earlier, I recalled being escorted by a friend to a startup project located in a small bungalow in south Minneapolis. On a sunny day in May, I watched what was happening at the house from behind waist-high hurricane fencing surrounding it. I watched three men at work in the yard, sawing new boards of wood held steady on saw horses. Inside the small house four other men worked with the sawn wood, creating tables and bookcases. The men's disabilities were recognizable, either by their facial features or by their slow and deliberate behavior. The goal of the fledgling enterprise was to provide employment for the intellectually challenged.

I am embarrassed to write, on that day I had absolutely no appreciation of the serious problem devoted parents were attempting to solve for their children. Lindsay was not yet five. I was still in the stage of complete denial that any permanent disability would mark my daughter for life. I'd not even come close to considering that one day my adorable tyke might be walking in those men's footsteps. Not only hadn't I come close to the thought, I was shocked to have anyone else believe it was something that could ever concern either my daughter or me.

What I really wanted was to leave the scene as quickly and politely as possible and forget it. After that day, the recollection of what was called Opportunity Workshop never again entered my thoughts, until for Lindsay, at twenty-two, a job was of extreme importance.

In the interim of the sixteen years we'd been away, Opportunity Workshop grew successfully into a block-long building with state-of-the-art offices and large workrooms for outsourced assignments. Supported by parents, local citizens and city businesses, the facility served nearly 1,500 clients with disabilities at 32 vocational and residential sites in Minnesota's twin cities of Minneapolis and St. Paul.

Later named Opportunity Partners, because each client and the business community are considered "partners" in the organization's success, OP provides both paid employment for people with disabilities and needed services to businesses of the city.

In 2003, Opportunity Partners celebrated its 50th anniversary. As reported by a local newspaper, "the word disabled falls short." The news article continues, "According to employers of the employees with special needs, the autistic, Down syndrome, brain injured and otherwise challenged adults, such workers are highly reliable and productive. They help businesses make money."

Assembly line clients handle packaging, sorting and repetitive tasks outsourced to OP by local industries. Off-site jobs place clients in restaurants, hotels and in retail stores, depending on the client's capability.

Five mornings a week Lindsay was, and still is, driven to the OP main building. She tells us about her place of employment, wherever it may be, but our questions seeking the details of her work day usually meet with the answer, "It's hard to explain"

Lindsay earns her own money and has her own personal counselor at OP, as do all clients. Her first year was spent as a worker on an assembly line, packaging earphones and other items for a local airline. The following years' promotions included mail deliverer for OP's offices and work in a restaurant. A year later she was hired by a hotel as a chambermaid. That year was not only remarkable because of her promotion, but also because of the number of phone calls to me that the job generated.

"I was fired," Lindsay called me one night, extremely distraught. She wasn't used to taking orders or to the perfectionism required by her new job. Happily, she was re-hired the next day by an understanding employer because she was an OP referral. Her supervisor was generous in the time she devoted to added instruction and several times afterward Lindsay was named 'Employee of the Month.' She proudly displays the monogramed mug she was awarded on her dresser top. Whenever we visited the hotel, we were treated as honored guests, as "Lindsay's family." At OP these successes are called, "Success, One Step at a Time."

Just as Lindsay worked off-site, OP has other clients working in Supported Employment Teams. The teams are small groups of individuals working in the community, doing many different kinds of tasks such as professional light cleaning at sixty-five sites. On-site, assembly workers continue to package items for department stores, airlines, food companies and small businesses. For one national chain of stores, each worker on a team that filled an unusually large order of items received a certificate for exemplary achievement. Everyone at OP works together to provide the community with services.

Jan Amis Jessup

At Lindsay's location there are more than 500 employees, including clients and staff. At OP the disabled who are the participants are considered "clients." The majority of staff members are Direct Support Professionals, DSPs, who provide direct care and supervision to the people served. Payment for clients is either piece-rated or variable on the assembly line or hourly. Clients are encouraged to earn as much as they can and are promoted to more responsible positions as they are able, including positions on community Supported Employment Teams or independent community employment.

Lindsay's is also involved in a program called Learning Options. It includes classes such as reading, writing, basic math and money math. Geography class and Exploration class involve field trips in the community. Social Class teaches subjects such as 'Me and My Relationships.' Cooking Light, in a large on-site kitchen, is cooking instruction. Lindsay's best loved class is Coffee Talk. That class features frequenting a local coffee shop for snacks and cups of coffee with her staff counselor, Benjamin. Its purpose is to teach manners suitable in public situations.

Length of service at OP is acknowledged each year in a touching ceremony that recognizes the loyalty, courage and responsibility of its clients. Lindsay recently received her thirty-five year award. OP's website motto is "Everyone When Given the Opportunity Adds Value to our World."

—◆・I◆I・◆—

During Bill's tenure as Director, a fourth structure, Cottage Four, was added to the CLI complex, a standard bungalow for six higher-functioning women. Lindsay moved to Cottage Four to live with women also employed by Opportunity Partners.

Stories of Lindsay's life in Cottage Four include her daily phone calls to the family describing the latest happenings. We marvel at the skill and understanding of staff members who work with the innocence and idiosyncrasies of six women living

"Will I Be on Television?"

together. Unexpected circumstances add to the fascinating narratives we receive from Lindsay, telling of her life in Cottage Four. One of our family's favorites is of the guileless, touching naiveté of a bitter-sweet situation involving a beau, and Lindsay's solution of the problem he unwittingly caused.

At times the women in Cottage Four traded beaus. Jane, one of Lindsay's house-mates, had two boyfriends that she met at OP. Lindsay had none. According to Jane, she "didn't need" both boyfriends. So, with generosity and grace at an OP annual dinner, Jane introduced Lindsay to one of them, named Jeffrey. Jeffrey took quite a fancy to Lindsay and after a while secretly gave her a small gold ring. The secret was well-kept, for Lindsay feared the staff would make her give it back. She was quite correct.

But during one of my visits to CLI, for Lindsay's *Annual* meeting, she shared her secret. She wanted advice. It seemed that all proceeded smoothly with Jeffrey until Jane decided she wanted him back. The problem was that Jeffrey didn't appreciate being a chess piece, to be moved from one girlfriend to another at whim. In addition, he was still quite taken with Lindsay. They were having good times together. Lindsay shared her worries with me over dinner one night. Frequently, it is difficult for her to put complicated thoughts into the longer sentences they sometimes require. So, her conversation began in her manner of using only a few words.

"Jane's mad at me," she said.

"Why is Jane mad at you? You've been friends for a long time," I said.

"Because"

"Because why?"

"She won't talk to me."

"Does Jane talk to the other girls?"

"Yes."

"Did you do something that made Jane mad?"

"Sort of," she said.

It took a while longer and quite a few more questions for me to discover that the problem was named Jeffrey and that the triangle romance was causing quite a stir in Cottage Four. Jeffrey's attention was making Lindsay happy, but she didn't know how to handle the troubles she was having with Jane. They worried her greatly.

"How much do you like Jeffrey?" I asked her after learning the whole story.

"Jane's mad at me." Lindsay was far more concerned about Jane's behavior than she was about Jeffrey. We talked several times more during my visit and Lindsay decided it was best to return the ring as quietly as she'd received it. As it turned out, Jeffrey, quite the ladies' man, simply moved on to greener pastures and found another girlfriend who didn't live at CLI. Peace reigned once again in Cottage Four. The beaus continued to be traded and soon both Lindsay and Jane had other male friendships at OP. That was the story's happy ending.

———◆·ı◆ı·◆———

Working with the county and state, Community Living and Opportunity Partners offer a variety of services. Through the forethought of the founders of each organization, additional dedicated personnel to improve the quality of life and keep things running smoothly were sought. Along with staff members, adjunct personnel includes Lindsay's OP employment counselor, a county nurse, social worker, psychologist and, by extension, medical specialists and whomever else is necessary to improve CLI's clients' welfare. There is a strong relationship with government professionals and private physicians practicing in the area. In an industry where staff turnover and retention is challenging, CLI has employees who have been in direct service to the company for 10, 20 and 30+ years! OP, as well, has long-term staff members and years of support from the families that began the project.

"Will I Be on Television?"

Forty-one years later as an admired asset to its surrounding town, CLI remains a town landmark; remarkable for meeting the needs of its clients with the training, employment partnership and the multitude of services it offers.

A highlight of Lindsay's year is her individual *Annual Meeting*. It can be attended by as many as ten who have direct care of the CLI client. It includes representatives of Opportunity Partners.

Those directly associated with her participate. The Client Care Director, Angie, whom I call Lindsay's Special Angel and second mother, is the "go to" person whenever the need arises. Angie, who has served all of the CLI clients for thirty-one years, directs the meeting. Also attending will be the permanent house parents, weekend house parents, adjunct staff members and Lindsay's employment counselor at Opportunity Partners. The participant's individual schedules are frequently overflowing, so the *Annual* meeting date must be set long in advance.

Lindsay's *'Annual'* is a professional review of her year from everyone's point of view. For Lindsay, it's her report card. So, from the time Lindsay learns the date, she agonizes far in advance, fearing she won't measure up. At the meeting, she reigns at the head of a long table, an honor that thrilled her when she became adept enough to hold that position. Still, acting as leader of the meeting is a privilege she rarely uses, unless she's asked a question or her opinion is sought. Mostly, she listens carefully to those attending as each person presents both a verbal and written report.

The meeting is a valuable tool. We're all given an opportunity to speak, to question and to resolve whatever issues may have arisen during the preceding year. I marvel at the extent of care my daughter receives. Those present not only keep Lindsay's interests in mind, they are in regular contact with me. Lindsay and every other participant must be well-satisfied when the meeting is concluded.

No matter how long it takes, each item brought up is discussed until a suitable plan results. Either a solution has been forthcoming or a problem will be carefully looked into and a solution will be found soon after the meeting. Following it, a 'Vocational/Educational Action Plan' is written, signed and distributed to everyone involved.

I've frequently summed up our mutual good fortune with this amazing facility by saying, "As I look around the table during Lindsay's *Annual*, I ponder, *Had I this many people caring for me, every day of my life, I wouldn't have a worry in the world.*

Community Living, Inc. and Opportunity Partners serve clients with many levels of special needs and those with diverse diagnoses. The facilities continue to earn high marks as a fine example of providing dedicated attention to detail—regarding the physical, mental and emotional needs—of each adult with developmental disabilities who is in their care. State, county and donor support make this level of success possible.

"Did You Know Lindsay Has a Heart Murmur?"

Lindsay, at twenty-two — or as she would say, "I am twenty-two years of age"—continued to be the combination of budding adult and naïve child. Her short stature, slightly less than five feet, was a blessing in one way. It made her appear considerably younger than her age. Consequently, in our world less was expected of her. In another way, despite her size, she began to carve a feisty but comfortable niche in the world of Community Living and Opportunity Partners. To Lindsay, her world was the normal world and she blossomed.

Her blossoming adult approach and appearance caught me unaware until one of my visits. I picked her up at OP after a work day. She stood chatting with co-workers. I had to look twice to recognize it was Lindsay who looked more adult and poised than I remembered from my last visit a few months earlier. As we talked in the car, her conversation took a more adult approach to her work assignment. It was unexpected and impressive.

At the same time, it was Lindsay's child-like self that delighted us with her love of Disney World, the Christmas holiday, new friends, birthday surprise parties and "lots of presents." Her spontaneous little girl reactions encouraged our desire to create happy times for her.

Our family's move back to Minnesota brought us back to close friends who also became relatives through marriage. Betty became Lindsay's aunt and Betty's twin brother and his wife, Bob and Lucille, were especially dear to the four of us, particularly Lindsay. "Uncle Bob" was the only one she permitted to call her anything but Lins. For "Uncle Bob," and only for him—a tease but a loving one—she answered to "Linslee." They had wonderful times with "Linslee" teasing Bob right back. They were both very funny whenever they were together.

Lucille stood in as my surrogate when I couldn't attend a few of Lindsay's special occasions. The occasion of my daughter's 35-year pin award from Opportunity Partner stands out as one heartbreaking time I couldn't be with my daughter. What saved the day was that Lindsay's favorite "Aunt Lucille" was by her side. Polly, Betty's daughter, who became Lindsay's cousin because of my marriage, could not be more dear or sweet to my daughter if she were her sister.

By 1975, Lindsay was well cared for at CLI by both Cary and Bill who were house parents in one of the cottages. At twenty-two she was sailing along without a care. She was healthy and happy. Her days were filled with intriguing projects at OP that boosted her self-confidence and she was kept busy by new friends. We felt comfortable leaving her in other hands and moving to Florida. Any concerns I had for Lindsay's well-being were allayed because of her excellent care. Still, as she grew past her twenties, the dire predictions of her pediatrician, about her heart valve not closed, and a shortened life, continued to cast their dark shadow.

A traumatic series of events reawakened all my fears with a bang. One entirely unexpected phone call forced me to relive the terrifying details surrounding the prospect of Lindsay's early death. I remembered the indecision of those earlier years and the relief I'd finally felt by not being forced to make a life or death decision for her. My relief evaporated with that phone call.

"Will I Be on Television?"

Winter in Florida is warm and balmy enough for lounging in a bathing suit at the edge of a swimming pool with not a care in the world. I was thoroughly enjoying the afternoon relaxing by our pool when I heard the phone ring. I roused myself from my serenity to walk into the house to answer and I was astounded to hear a man's voice barking, almost loud enough to be heard from Minneapolis to Florida without benefit of a phone. "Did you know your daughter has a heart murmur?"

Why was this man shouting at me? Had something terrible happened to my daughter? I panicked, especially when the man at the other end of the phone identified himself as Lindsay's doctor in Minneapolis. Had my indecision about her heart problem wreaked a catastrophe? My thoughts raced back to the valve in her heart that didn't close at birth. I felt as if I were re-living the reprise of a bad movie. In my mind I again heard her pediatrician's words, "If her heart valve is not surgically closed before she is twelve, her life expectancy will be no longer than twenty or twenty-one years. Her heart will slowly wind down like an unwound clock."

But when she was a baby, her pediatrician didn't recommend surgery. So, I'd planned for Lindsay to have the operation in eight or ten years. When she was eight, I questioned doctors again. Her pediatrician was against heart surgery. Our family doctor wouldn't consider an operation. Though their reasons were unspoken, I believed it was because of Lindsay's mental problems. Or it may have been that their concern was the same as mine, would her life become extremely difficult if she lived to old age?

I don't remember asking that doctor who was calling me if Lindsay was all right. I must have, for he reassured me. "Lindsay's all right, but she *must* have heart surgery."

Heart surgery?! At that moment I dared to hope that none of my drastic imaginings were true. Was it possible that we were being offered another chance? A doctor finally seemed to want

Lindsay's life to be extended. Could it be that Lindsay and I had someone in our corner at last?

Still startled by his angry accusation, I'd had the impulse to shout back, "Of course! I certainly know that my daughter has a heart murmur." But when his voice calmed, I calmed, too. It seemed necessary to explain the history of Lindsay's heart problem and of the medical advice I'd received for years. I told him her story from the beginning, explaining that when my daughter was a tyke I'd agreed with the doctors I consulted. "At the time heart surgery presented dangers, especially for a handicapped child who couldn't understand what was happening to her," I said. "Lindsay faced enough challenges. But as she remained healthy and her ability to understand improved, I'd struggled with the weighty decision."

I explained that for twelve years I lived with questions. "Would medical opinion have been different for a child without Lindsay's handicap?" I'd had other questions about her future welfare. When my daughter became an adult, would she face problems she couldn't handle because of her disability? Had the doctors been trying to tell me that a short happy life for my daughter would be better than a longer one that could be fraught with difficulty? And, who would care for Lindsay if something happened to me?

This doctor was courteous enough to listen patiently as I described Lindsay breezing through her first twelve years giving no hint that her life or early death depended on the judgment I'd struggled over for years.

"When she turned twelve she was healthy and thriving," I said. "Our family doctor still remained firmly against heart surgery. A decision eluded me. By procrastinating, I convinced myself that *what was meant to be would be. Lindsay's life was in more powerful hands than mine.*"

The doctor's voice became pleasant after hearing my explanation. Still, he repeated, "She must have heart surgery." He was

"Will I Be on Television?"

insistent, though he went out of his way to calm my fears about any immediate problem.

"Do you really mean that it's not too late?" I wanted to believe what I was hearing even though it contradicted everything I'd been told for years.

"It isn't too late." His words were a gift, far greater than he could have known.

Still, practicality took over. "Will the surgery be dangerous?" I didn't know the man. I had to be sure of what he was telling me. I had to be certain I wasn't endangering my daughter on someone's whim. For so long, I'd been instilled with the medical information that she must have her heart surgery by the time she was twelve years old. "Will you give me a little time to gather my thoughts?" I asked. He'd calmed considerably and agreed.

Just as in the past, after the doctor's call responsibility for the decision about Lindsay's life rested with me alone.

For years, since Lindsay was twelve and I believed I'd made an important decision, I'd felt relief. I'd had many fewer sleepless nights because of concerns for Lindsay. She was healthy. She was happy. She was well cared for. I'd felt secure moving away because we were in close touch. That night I couldn't sleep because of my excitement; a closed door had opened in an unexpected and wonderful way. I was too elated over the possibility of saving Lindsay from what could be a premature death. Still, common sense told me that there were too many ramifications for quick answers.

Buddy, my considerate and cautious husband stayed up with me and we talked. The next morning I phoned our family doctor to tell him about the call and seek information about the doctor who had called me. Our doctor had been in practice in Minneapolis for years. He knew our family well and had known Lindsay for most of her life. We were comfortable with each other and could talk honestly. I brought him up-to-date regarding Lindsay's present situation and told him of the doctor's phone call. He didn't know the doctor who called me. "I'll do some research and call you back," he said.

The following day he returned my call. After checking, he didn't question the credentials of Lindsay's doctor. But his reaction and comments were shocking. He counseled against Lindsay's having surgery just as he had for years. Older, he remained firm in the more traditional frame of mind. I questioned whether the call from Lindsay's younger doctor might be the result of cultural change in attitudes toward the intellectually disabled. Or was it surgical progress making the operation safer. That question was never entirely answered.

Facing two diametrically opposing opinions threw me into the painful web of indecision once more. Again, I felt that I was being asked to play God. For three days the decision about whether or not to put Lindsay through the necessary surgery weighed so heavily on my mind that I could think of nothing else. I still remember those days too well. Much of the time I didn't know what I was doing. I was in such a daze that my actions were entirely automatic.

Amazingly, as suddenly as the indecision began it ended. I was in our swimming pool trying to clear my mind, treading water, struggling and puzzling, agonizing over what decision to make for my daughter's future. When, as miraculous as it still seems, the answer came with my feeling a literal bolt from the blue, almost like a lightening strike. Immediately, I knew, without doubt, that I could no longer procrastinate and take the chance that Lindsay might die too soon.

My relief was tremendous. Our Easter child had been truly blessed. For several moments I felt the peace that, indeed, passes all understanding. My gratitude for this second chance to safely extend my daughter's life was overwhelming. Two days later, Lindsay's heart surgery was scheduled.

The following week I flew to Minneapolis to tell Lindsay that she would be going to a hospital for a short time. It was an extended visit to prepare her and to talk with her about what she could expect. With her usual short sentences she asked many questions. The first was, "Will I die?" I searched for the right words to reassure her, in terms she'd understand and not be fearful. My answer was to reach back to a happy past experience for comparison. Years earlier in the East, Lindsay was hospitalized with serious flu. Staff members of the local small hospital went out of their way to make her "Queen for a day." Her four day's experience had been a good one. Lindsay has an excellent memory and hadn't forgotten. "You didn't die that time," I told her. "You won't die this time."

Still, she had more questions than I anticipated. "What will happen to me?" she asked. I explained the procedures as simply as possible without alarming details. Many times, she asked me for that explanation over again.

Many more times she asked, "Will I die?" That was an easy question to keep answering with certainty, though I'm not sure that Lindsay was entirely convinced.

"I'll be with you the whole time," I reassured her. "You'll be fine." This became one of the times when it was important to acknowledge the "child" still present in my daughter's twenty-two year old mind. A teddy bear to take to the hospital soothed her. By the scheduled time, she seemed to understand and was ready for her hospital stay, with new pajamas, bunny slippers and a shiny overnight case for important accompaniments.

"Am I being brave?" she touchingly asked me often. Her bravery was reinforced by members of the hospital staff from the minute she walked in the front door. I could not have anticipated the attention and kindness she received in that community hospital. Just as during her earlier hospitalization, "Miss Lindsay" quickly became Queen of her miniature kingdom, with scads of visitors, cards and gifts! Following her surgery and comparatively quick recovery, she was almost sorry to leave the hospital when it was time to go home to Community Living and her friends.

We couldn't have asked for a happier outcome to what probably would have been a far shorter life had that doctor not acted.

Though Lindsay's physical ability didn't change following her surgery, I changed. The fear for her that I'd carried for so many years lifted, bringing me remarkable relief.

"Cary, I'm in Trouble"

At twenty-three years, Lindsay began showing signs of teenage rebellion. I recalled once again that having a special needs child can be a roller coaster ride.

Lindsay's early years came back to me as if they were the rerun of an old black and white television show. At about four-and-a-half years, unexpected symptoms of her brain damage appeared, seeming to pop up overnight. I had no choice but to accept what I'd fought for so long. My daughter might never be considered "normal." Lindsay developed symptoms I could no longer ignore.

Help came as unexpectedly as Lindsay's symptoms. A doctor I didn't know heard about her problems from a mutual friend. He phoned me, describing an experimental project. "A Swiss company is testing new medications. They call these drugs tranquilizers," he said. "Would you be interested in having your daughter participate?" Since I was desperate to try anything that would help Lindsay, I immediately agreed to bring her to his downtown office.

At four-and-a-half, Lindsay loved dressing up and riding in cars, so the visit to the doctor's office seemed like a great adventure. She played with her doll while I listened to his description of the research.

"Mellaril," he said, is a new product of a Swiss pharmaceutical firm. It's one of the first drugs known as tranquilizers." The doctor explained that the medication would affect the damaged portion of Lindsay's brain to better allow the undamaged parts to become stronger. When I asked for more specific details, the doctor was reluctant to answer. He said, "Please let me know what results you observe." He wanted written records of her responses and told me that he would periodically test her reactions. With nothing to lose, I agreed that Lindsay would participate. He handed me papers to complete and gave Lindsay her first pill with a glass of water.

Three hours later, at home, the change in my daughter was startling…almost too amazing to believe.

The medication (thioridizine hcl) continued to make a remarkable difference. Mellaril immediately became part of Lindsay's medication routine, uninterrupted until she was in her late twenties.

But at 23 years during her delayed teenage rebellion she became quite difficult, not only with her housemates but at work, as well. She complained frequently to the CLI and OP staff members and particularly to me during her long distance calls home.

"Carol did (whatever it happened to be that day) to me," she'd complain. She found fault with her jobs and co-workers. Her OP counselor moved her from one assignment to another attempting to satisfy her. "They picked on me," she'd tell me. When I asked "how" or "why," she'd say, "I can't explain it," or "let's not talk about it."

We never knew what to expect. This is one conversation during that time. Lindsay called Cary on a Friday afternoon.

"Cary, I'm in trouble."

"Why?" Cary asked.

"I got fired today."

"So what else is new?"

"Well, you know how Mom is coming from Florida to my award ceremony next week. It's for five years. Now, I can't go."

"What did you do?" Cary asked.

"I tore up my paycheck."

"Will I Be on Television?"

"Who did that hurt, Lins?"

"Me."

But of course, Lins was back at work Monday and the award ceremony, with me in attendance, went off without a hitch.

It was impressive to learn how many staff members from both CLI and Opportunity Partners attempted to help my daughter during this challenging stage of her young adult life. It also was impressive to learn of the dedication of both organizations' staff members. This was particularly true since any employment for those with developmental disabilities was rare in the country at that time. Still there are many fewer positions than there are adults with developmental disabilities who would like to work. One of the most difficult challenges for people with special needs is finding any available activity, even instruction, after they become twenty-two years old. Not only did Lindsay have jobs, she was earning her own money and increasing her skills by working at these various assignments.

The Community Living staff's solutions for Lindsay's problems included frequent counseling appointments with a psychologist and the addition of the anti-depressant medication Zoloft to her daily dosage of Mellaril. Although it wasn't immediate, eventually the combination of counseling and the addition of Zoloft improved her disposition noticeably.

At about the same time, and after years of Mellaril's widespread use, potential long-term side effects of Thioridizine hcl (generic for Mellaril) were being discovered. Lindsay had no symptoms, but others showed adverse reactions including depression and suicidal thoughts. The County nurse's edict was that Lindsay's dosage of Mellaril should be discontinued. Lindsay's history of success with the medication and my spoken concerns didn't carry enough weight to be able to avoid their discontinuing her Mellaril.

This, of course, explained Lindsay's immediately apparent changed behavior. Quickly, she began to relapse into her former obstinacy and angry outbursts. With no signs of improvement the Community Living staff agreed that the change in Lindsay's behavior was too obvious to overlook. With my signature as Lindsay's Conservator we were able to get her dosage reduced rather than eliminated.

A year later, the County Health Department received more disturbing notices of side effects of the medication. A sterner edict was received by CLI and Lindsay's use of Mellaril was again discontinued. I was given no notice of this change, nor any opportunity to object to the decision. The CLI staff also disagreed with the edict in Lindsay's case because of their past experience with her. But they had no choice.

As a result, Lindsay's constant angry phone calls home began again. They were filled with furious tirades about her latest problem. Previously, even at her worst, she'd never had such a fierce temper. I was puzzled and worried by her extreme backsliding. Cary was aware of it, too, since she was receiving the same kinds of calls from her sister. Neither of us knew how to deal with Lindsay's worsening regression.

Hoping a vacation with us might help Lindsay's unhappiness, Cary and I planned a four-day weekend with her at Disney World in Florida. But when we got to the park she was still unlike the happy person we'd known for most of her years. She was non-compliant and argumentative. She angrily refused to go on some rides. She was hesitant about getting into the rolling cars and going into dark tunnels. She said, "I'm afraid," and refused to go on those rides. She also had trouble climbing into the moving cars because the time allowed for their stopping for entry was too brief for her coordination. She'd hang tight onto our arms if we tried to help her. She'd dig her heels in hard and refuse to budge. We noticed that her coordination had worsened.

We sought out rides that catered to younger children's needs. We also let her choose the restaurants she might like. After the first day, and lots of adjustments, the three of us began having a much better time. In fact, Lindsay didn't want to go home. She didn't want to leave the Magic Kingdom.

She became increasingly balky and angry when we told her it was time to leave. We couldn't stay longer because our hotel reservations were at their end. She refused to behave when we packed. She threw her clothes into her suitcase so that I had to catch and fold them to be able to close the bag. She dug in her heels when it was time to go to the hotel lobby and to my car. I'd never before seen Lindsay like this and was puzzled, mentally searching for a reason. Cary and I took each of her arms and led her toward the elevator while the bellman carried the luggage. She plunked herself down on the carpet in the middle of the hallway.

"What on earth are you doing? We'd like to stay, too, but we can't. We must go home NOW!," I told her. But no amount of explaining or insistence worked. We pulled her to her feet and struggled to get her into the elevator and seated on a bench in the lobby. She did remain seated while we waited for the keys to my car, but when the bellman brought them she realized we really were leaving and erupted again. She had a furious temper tantrum followed by tears. "I won't go." She screeched in a loud angry voice. An audience of a few curious souls couldn't help watching. It was easy to imagine their thinking, "What are those awful women doing to that poor handicapped child?"

"She's had such a good time that she doesn't want to leave," I meekly attempted to explain some who were standing nearby. "She's usually not like this." Why do I think they didn't believe me?

When my car arrived at the double doors, Cary held one of Lindsay's arms while I hustled her into the passenger seat. I held her in her seat until Cary could close the door without pinching her. We had two cars because Cary had driven separately from her home on Florida's West Coast. While Cary waited for her car, I drove Lindsay away before anything else could happen. As I pulled away from the hotel as fast and as I safely could, I talked to Lindsay, attempting to calm her down. For a while she seemed better. It wasn't until we got to the open highway that she started again with a slow anger that grew like a boiler working up a head of steam. "I'm NOT going home," she shouted, repeating it many times over.

Those were the years before seat belts. There were no restraints in cars. Lindsay angrily thrashed around in the passenger seat, shouting between tears. Driving at sixty-five, the speed limit, seemed fast in those days, but I wanted to get where we were going as quickly as possible. I was trying to pacify her with words when I saw her reach for her door handle. Her car door opened. Caught by the wind the door flew open wide and pulled her half way from her seat. With one hand on the wheel I reached for her with the other and grabbed her shirt—or her skirt. I can't remember what I grabbed, but it held her in the car until I could slow and pull over to side of the road. Her door was still open when the car stopped on the shoulder. I was trembling and Lindsay was frightened, too.

She understood what happened. She may not have realized what could have happened to her. I went around the rear of the automobile, settled her in her seat, closed her door and locked it, pushing down the button. For the rest of the drive she was quiet.

She remained with me at home for two comparatively calm days until it was time for her to return to CLI. Upon her return I spoke at length with Angie and learned that Lindsay's Mellaril had been discontinued. I could think of no other reason for her unusual behavior, and I turned into a squeakier wheel than ever before. As a result, with my semi-annual signature and because of the car episode, Lindsay's return to her former dosage of the medication was assured.

"Will I Be on Television?"

Since that time other psychotropic medications have come to the market. Lindsay continues to take Melarill, but her prescription for Zoloft has been replaced with a different and newer medication.

"Surprise Me"

*L*indsay's 53rd to 55th years made me write this book. At her 53rd birthday party with the family gathered around, Lindsay made an unexpected pronouncement that precipitated a merry-go-round of fun. Bent on immediate action, she forged ahead, brooking no naysaying, permitting no interruptions or questions.

"In two years I will be 55 years of age and I want a *BIG* birthday party," she announced. Thus began her painstaking planning of the party, exactly as she wanted it. While eating her birthday cake at the 53rd year party, she described the 55th year cake. "Ice cream cake, chocolate with whipped cream on top." She made sure we wrote down the date…. just as if we hadn't known it for 53 years. "I want it to be April 5th, my 55th birthday." she said. "Four o'clock in the afternoon. Dinner,too." She went on to plan the menu, accepting only a very few suggestions from the gathered group.

Lindsay planned the location. "I want it here, at your house," she told me. Next came the guest list, the entertainment. "Balloons," she said. She finished with a verbal exclamation point, "LOTS and LOTS of PRESENTS!" She made sure that Cary, Bruce and I had our precise marching orders.

I must admit to our being taken aback by this list of exacting requirements. As we listened to what Lindsay described, her presentation was accompanied by our shared incredulity and rolled eyes. The event sounded like a full blown Broadway production, complete with cast, costumes and scenery, all planned to the last detail. Then came the bombshell: "*I want it to be a Surprise Party!*"

Once again, as it had so often in the past, our family's laughter and fun began at that moment because of Lindsay. The three of us knew we'd go far out of the way to fulfill all the child-like wishes that continued to be a part of our adult Lindsay. But how, on earth, does a surprise party come about when the guest-of-honor has planned everything in advance? We began two years' of our own planning behind the scenes. Still, since she'd conceived her party to the last detail, how could we possibly surprise her? Simple, we plotted, schemed and lied.

There were other times we plotted, schemed and lied to make sure that Lindsay got what she wanted. During Lindsay's Florida visits she charmed those we knew well. Our Christmas Eve dinners included family, good friends and guests who didn't have their own family members near for the holidays.

After these dinners, we'd adjourn to the living room for dessert, coffee and to play a game known as a "Chinese Auction." Each one of us brought a wrapped silly gift for under the Christmas tree. Each one received a number. Number One selected a gift and opened it.

Number Two selected a different gift. Or, not in the Christmas spirit, stole the gift that Number One was holding. Laughter always ensued.

But while the rest of us played the game with some level of "seriousness," two of our group hatched their own plans. Making no attempt to be coy about the gift they wanted, Lindsay and our very special long-time friend, Bob, made it abundantly clear which gift they thought was theirs. Much more laughter. And, of course, we "The Serious" made sure that Lindsay and Bob received their gifts.

"Will I Be on Television?"

Lindsay was particularly adept at the game. The Christmas Eve that an extra-large caramel apple showed up among the early gifts, she could barely contain herself. She was wide-eyed when her turn did not come up and someone else nabbed the apple (of course, meaning to make sure Lindsay got it). But Lindsay didn't know that.

Soon it was Lindsay's turn. With several more numbers after hers…all in the hands of other "thieves," (she felt sure)….she pounced on that apple. She tore out of the living room as fast as she could, ran right upstairs to her bedroom and shut the door behind her.

◆ • I ◆ I • ◆

Our annual Christmas guests became the first on the "surprise party" list. Jack, my life companion since I lost my husband, is one of Lindsay's and our family's favorites. Each time Lindsay phones she asks about Jack. Many times he's nearby so they talk frequently. He is wonderful with her.

Nancy, Bob's wife, is exceptionally considerate. She rearranges her schedule to be sure to see Lindsay when my daughter is in town. She diligently shops for the special kinds of gifts she knows will please Lindsay.

Jan McArt, the First Lady of Florida Theater, also puts the utmost thought into gifts for Lindsay. The clock ring from Jan is one of Lindsay's most treasured possessions. For years, Lindsay had a front-row seat at the Dinner Theater Jan founded. Jan also slipped away from other parties when Lindsay was visiting just so she wouldn't miss their time together.

Roxy, whom I met in Washington, D.C. through the League of American Orchestras, is another one of Lindsay's devoted friends. We have spent many memorable Thanksgivings with Roxy and her family. Between family gatherings, Roxy is in close touch with what Lindsay is doing.

One summer Barb met Lindsay in a Northern Wisconsin restaurant where live goats feed on the roof. During that almost three-hour breakfast of delicious Swedish pancakes, Barb and Lindsay became super-buddies.

These friends, and others, show their love for Lindsay in countless ways. When you have a special needs child you realize that there is a minority of people who are truly altruistic with their contributions to your child's happiness. Our family gives them heartfelt thanks.

The poet, William Wordsworth, put it well: "The best portion of a good man's life is his little, nameless, unremembered acts of kindness and of love."

Lindsay was included in the fun of our party planning. She became the source and originator of not only daily family phone calls, but of our constant hilarity about *"I want it to be a surprise party."* With each of her calls, first to me, then from Lindsay to Cary and Bruce and from them circling back to me, our fun and laughter grew, and this book began to take shape in my mind.

My "social worker" musing about a book that would share resources and hope with parents of other children who had special needs, fostered an unexpected realization about my own daughter. I wondered why it hadn't occurred to me years earlier. Lindsay, whom the doctors and others in our family were ready to put away in some God forsaken institution and pretend she'd never been born, has become one of our mainstays.

Lindsay, who some would consider the least contributor to a family was the one responsible for most of our mutual communications. If her sister, brother and I are the spokes of the family wheel, Lindsay is the hub. The four of us live in different cities. Lindsay's calls are what keep all of us in close touch. Lindsay is the one who friends and relatives gather around when she has a special occasion to celebrate. Lindsay, loving us all uncondition-

"Will I Be on Television?"

ally, unconcerned about what we do or are, simply wants to know we're there for her and she wants to be with us every chance she has. Her daily calls delight us, whether about planning her party or simply telling us the events of her days.

At sometime, during the next two years of party planning, Cary nicknamed her sister *"The Great Manipulator."* For instance, when the *Manipulator* is bent on visiting, she'll ask me, "Can I come to Florida and visit Cary?"

"Fine with me," I'll tell her. "But you'd better ask Cary. See if it fits her work schedule." The next call to Cary goes something like this. "Mom said I should visit you. When can I come?" Then, of course, Cary calls me and asks, "Did you tell Lindsay she could come (at such and such a time) to visit me?" and a visit to her sister and to me are the result.

If Lindsay has nothing to plan, ask or report when she calls, she'll tease with her favorite rhetorical questions, often repeated, "Can I drive a car?" or "Can I get married?" knowing she'll do neither. We know that she finds great fun in our answers, listening to us brush off her questions with platitudes that won't hurt her feelings like "Can you afford to buy a car?"

At least that is what I thought about her "Can I get married?" question, until the time Cary phoned me to say, "I'm going to be the Maid of Honor in a wedding."

"How nice, dear. Who's getting married?" I asked, unsuspecting.

"Lindsay is."

"*WHAT?!*" from me. It was the time that the six ladies in Lindsay's cottage were trading boyfriends. Recall that a boyfriend, who wasn't being used by another resident, was given to Lindsay. He fell in love with my daughter and secretly gave her a ring. The match was touching, but bittersweet, for nothing could come of it. Neither Lindsay nor the man could undertake serious responsibility. Nor did they want to. So, Lindsay was not disappointed by the outcome of simply remaining friends. As so many times in the past, I appreciated my daughter's acceptance of her life.

I realized, once again, that Lindsay had never been bitter or angry because of what she didn't have. She'd never questioned, "Why me?" She'd courageously made the best of her place in this world.

When the party planning began in earnest, closer to the date, we talked to each other more often. To me Lindsay would request, "Have Cary call me." To Cary she'd say, "Tell *your mother* to get my plane ticket to Florida." From Bruce she'd want to know, "Are you and Missie and Allie and Ames coming to my birthday party?" Of course, the three of us would then call each other about her questions or requests. At the same time we'd share the news of each of our lives.

This is the round-robin in our family members that has endured for years because of Lindsay. The only difference in our calls was whatever fit the goings-on at the moment. But during the party planning Lindsay's role as News Editor-in-Chief became even more carved in stone.

At first, we laughed a lot about the party, still wondering how to fulfill her request for a *surprise*. So, we planned surprises within the party. Bruce, his wife, two children and Bob Barker, their dog, would arrive after Bruce's repeatedly telling Lindsay they couldn't make it. Lindsay and their daughter, Allyne, have a special bond. Allie detours far out of her way to have dinner with Lindsay whenever she's traveling anywhere in the vicinity.

Another *surprise* would be the presence of Jack's two daughters, Marcy and Carla, who Lindsay loves. It never entered her mind that they would fly in for the occasion from their out-of-state homes hundreds of miles across the country.

"Will I Be on Television?"

What to do about invitations? She'd know if we invited friends that were to be part of her *surprise*. The solution was to have Lindsay choose her invitations from samples I sent. Six weeks before the party I sent her a package of addressed and sealed stamped envelopes. That way one of her house-parents could take the unopened package of invitations to the post office for her.

Once we came up with that solution we faced an even greater obstacle. For a long time we pondered, *how does one manage to have a surprise party for a guest of honor who planned the entire event?* That solution was a long time coming. Finally, the best answer was the easiest. We'd simply have her party the day before her birthday. If we surprised her when she least expected it and all her other aspirations were met, we hoped she would be so happy the date wouldn't matter. The rest of our secrets surprised even us. They fell into place perfectly.

Three days before her birthday, Lindsay traveled to Florida. Two days later, the morning of the party, she was spirited from my home by one of my friends with the treat of pre-birthday shopping. Quickly, the requested Happy Birthday banners were hung, balloons were tied to door knobs and bannisters. Marcy and Carla, still a *surprise,* sat on the living room floor wrapping many separate gifts from a pile of small ones like note pads, pencils, a pretty shower cap, so Lindsay would have "lots of presents" to open.

The sound system beamed her favorite Beatles music. At four in the afternoon all was in readiness, just as the birthday girl ordered. Decades earlier, had I agreed with the doctors who recommended hiding Lindsay in an institution, the day of my excited daughter's 55th birthday party would never have arrived.

"Here she comes. Quiet everyone, until she's at the door," Cary's hushed tone spilled over the room. My front door opened.

Loud and in unison thirty-eight voices shouted, "*Surprise!*" Lindsay's eyes opened wide. Her guests watched her face glow with the startled rapture of her smile, as she said sweetly and with her usual innocence, "I *really* was surprised." Every expression in the room reflected her enchantment. Quite a few had lumps in their throats or watery eyes.

"She makes us all better people," a friend said. "It's touching to watch someone who has to work so hard to make her way in this world be so happy." Mulling over similar comments and watching my daughter laughing, teasing with her brother, posing for pictures and thrilled beyond anything we might have imagined, I had tugs at my heart many times that day.

Later that evening Cary pulled a chair up to help her sister stand on it to reach over the table top. She tenderly encouraged Lindsay to blow out her birthday candles and make a wish. Their mutual devotion could not have been more apparent. "Look at her," Cary whispered in my ear. "She's having a wonderful time.

That day belonged to Lindsay from beginning to end. But it belonged to everyone else, as well. Once again, we fell in love with the star of our show.

Fifty-five years earlier, Lindsay was considered by doctors to be the *least* able to contribute to a family. The *least* turned out to be the *best* for the rest of us. Recently a wise doctor said to me, "A family who has a special needs child has someone who is very special." That day his words described everyone's feelings perfectly.

Since that birthday Lindsay's had two more *surprise* parties, both intricately planned by herself. The latest was her 60th. She'd trained us well to orchestrate each event so she could truthfully say twice again, "I really was surprised."

There also have been *surprises* along the way. Surprises come in many forms, some devastating.

"Will I Be on Television?"

Lindsay was fifty before any doctor used the words "oxygen deprivation" to explain her brain damage. For years, common sense told me that was the reason. So, although I was pleased to have my conclusion confirmed, his words did not come as a surprise.

But as I described her stiffness and unresponsiveness the morning after she was hospitalized, this doctor backed off. Abruptly, he slammed the door shut on further conversation. He quickly moved across the room to talk to someone else. I was startled by his reaction. His behavior was the first surprise. *Five more years passed before the worst surprise.*

"Something happened overnight in the hospital."

Another doctor, in another state, used those words five years later. Once more my thoughts roared back to that horrifying morning when the nurse handed my baby to me. Was she the baby I'd trustingly given into the hospital staff's care the afternoon before? Not wanting to believe it was Lindsay, I checked the name tag on her wrist. It read Lindsay.

At long last, I understood why, with a very sick baby, I was spirited away to that bare and empty storeroom and left alone, with no doctor or nurse available. We were hidden in isolation.

That way, there would be no talk...no questions.

Of my three children, it is Lindsay who is most connected with the rest of us. Lindsay calls me daily, and Cary and Bruce almost as often, at the risk of being "talked to" about her "phone bills." Lindsay sends the most greeting cards. With help, Lindsay sends 'thank you' notes.

Cary's and Bruce's understanding and empathy were strengthened because of living with Lindsay. Their consideration for others who face challenges showed in their younger years and certainly in Cary's years as a teacher. Recently, when I asked Cary, "What's it been like to live with a special needs person in the family?"

"She's my sister." Her immediate simple answer says it all.

Now, after Lindsay's *second* self-planned *surprise party* as a sixty-year-old, she continues to direct her life with a masterful hand. Just as the founder of Community Living, Inc. dreamed, she lives in her suburban ranch cottage with five other (almost always) compatible women with disabilities. She's shepherded by a caring house-parent staff, Mike and Denise, along with Susan, a staff member on the weekend. They laugh and enjoy her sense of humor. Lindsay's health and well-being are overseen by a significant extended staff.

When Lindsay succeeds at her job at Opportunity Partners and gains a reward, lunch with her counselor, she sparkles with happiness. She calls us to say, "I had a good day." Her work earned her a handsome pin for 35 years of steady employment with Opportunity Partners.

When she has a complaint, she makes herself heard. Cary and I listen. If we ask a question, we must be prepared for a straight forward, to the point, honest answer. Lindsay is guileless. Often, we have no idea what to expect.

Lindsay's short stature, little girl lisp and innocent delight when she's pleased make her seem more like a pre-teen than the sixty-year-old adult she is. On the other hand, she flies cross-country by herself without a qualm. Happily she'll not be lost in the Chicago airport ever again. Not only does one airline fly non-stop from Minneapolis to Florida, the staff protects Lindsay from check-in to being met by a pre-registered person. A single phone call to Dawn, or another of her efficient co-workers at the airline, takes care of all arrangements.

"Will I Be on Television?"

Lindsay has enjoyed summers at camp and numerous trips with her friends under the auspices of Tours Exceptionale, an adjunct organization to Community Living. Her adjustment in a difficult world is as admirable as her courage in the face of the challenges she's conquered.

She is excited about 'her book.'

Now, her daily questions are not, "Can I drive a car?" or "Can I get married," but two different ones.

"Are you working on my book?" (in a tone of voice that says "for goodness sake get on with it,") and

"Will I be on television?"

A Journey of Experience, Education and Enlightenment

After a fifty-five-year learning curve about Lindsay's special needs, the curve rose exponentially as I began the fascinating journey of investigating and reporting for this book. Following leads, conducting interviews, doing medical research, talking with educators, parents, siblings, shirt-tail relatives and other special needs individuals, more than proved the vital need for sharing the helpful information I was gathering. Whenever I mentioned the subject of my book, interest increased as do ripples in a pool when a pebble is dropped into it.

No matter with whom I spoke, in every group someone had a related story to tell. At times the small groups included only four people.

In the 50's and 60's a family with a "mentally retarded" child faced a harsh stigma. An expression of the times was, "A blot on the family escutcheon." In truth, an intellectually disabled child was more than a mere "blot." Those children were hidden. Many were institutionalized. Adults rarely appeared in public. They were seldom, if ever, mentioned in conversation. During those years no one would have acknowledged such a family problem much less permitted their story to be included in a book.

A slowly growing improvement in attitude began in the '70s and in the years that followed, its thrust increased. Skip to 2008. A state Governor introduced her Down syndrome baby on national television. A television host talked about his child with special needs. A football great founded a summer camp for these youngsters. An autistic PhD, who works closely with animals, has written books and had a nationally lauded documentary about her work featured on television.

I learned about creative teachers. One was educated in a California Special Education school that assesses the entire child's needs, mental and physical, before determining the education plan that will promote their growth.

In Tuscaloosa, Alabama, Martha Cook, PhD. uses her years of Special Ed instruction wisely to combat the lack of acceptance of the intellectually disabled. Dr.Cook is the Director of the Rise pre-kindergarten school, affiliated with the University of Alabama, that mingles the Special Needs children with the other typically developing children. "The other children vie to befriend and take care of those with disabilities," she told me. "A child who is introduced to special needs children in pre-kindergarten," she said, "will grow up never being prejudiced."

Funding for resources is now provided by the federal government, states and counties. Nevertheless, much more is needed.

As an example, "It was the worst day of my life," a woman I met told me recently, "I knew something was wrong with my baby and I couldn't get a diagnosis. She was my adopted little girl. I had no idea of what to do. Where could I go for help?" She said, "I was frantic."

Another friend shared, "When the doctor told me, I didn't believe him. It felt like I was stepping into a black hole. I wanted to scream."

An experienced medical specialist told me, "There are doctors who will diagnose an autistic child, then say, "I'll see you in six weeks." She added, "Parents don't know where to turn or how or where to seek information. They feel that they're in a vacuum."

"Will I Be on Television?"

A banker, working with Special Needs trusts, tells, "Even now it takes parents a long time to talk about their child." This is in part because of fear of stigma but also because the parent has not accepted the fact that they have a special needs child.

Not one of these emotions is unfamiliar to me. I've experienced every one of them. Nevertheless, because of what I've seen and learned, because of my daughter and my research, I also can share the resources of *HELP* and I know that there can be *HOPE*.

My education began because of Lindsay's needs and learning about Sudden Infant Death Syndrome (SIDS). Now the medical community is rethinking SIDS, with the result that many deaths have been prevented and the disorder is no longer a mystery.

My experience continued with the founding and development of two outstanding facilities in Minnesota, Community Living, Incorporated, and Opportunity Partners. The success of each one is worth far more than a chapter. Each story is a guidebook. Each can be an excellent model to follow wherever daily living success, or activity and employment, is necessary for children and adults with special needs.

Much remains to be done. Some facilities are expensive and not covered by Medicaid or the Medicaid Waver. In some locations there are day programs. Still, too many adults with special needs are forced to stay at home all day. To be accepted for a long term care facility, they must have maladaptive behaviors that prevent their being cared for at home. However, progress is being made. Businesses are hiring persons with special needs and a few businesses have been started that specialize in employing persons with autism.

Before I began this book, I learned about Sam. Sam's grandfather, a university professor, impressed me six years ago as vastly different from the grandfathers of the 50s, even those of the 2000s. In an era when Special Needs was still stigmatized, he featured his ten-year-old grandson's progress on his website. How unusual was that?

"Sam, whose birth weight was one-and-a-half pounds, is overcoming all dire predictions," he wrote. Later, "Although Sam can't walk or talk, he's making connections." Still later, "Sam has achieved more in his life than anyone I know. Every time I see him, I see improvement." His e-mails continued throughout the years. Sam's saga highlighted the *hope* so needed by families. At sixteen, Sam is in a high school for disabled young people. He still neither walks nor talks in sentences. He has his own words to meet his needs, words for crackers, milk, doll. He sings with the Opera radio broadcasts on Saturdays and loves to play his electronic piano. He's happy and mischievous, though not always good.

I'll never forget the emotional depth of his Grandfather's words when we eventually met. He said, "I have a 140 IQ grandson and a 30 IQ grandson. The one excites and intrigues me. But the other, Sam, deeply touches me. Sam is wonderful. I enjoy them both at an entirely different level. That defines love."

Skylar was born to a good friend's daughter. Before Skylar was born, her grandmother, the mother of five, frequently hoped out loud for at least one grandchild. For her, it was far too long a time before her wish was fulfilled. So, by the time Skylar was a baby girl about to be born, there had been numerous showers, a layette representing every dream and an entire club's members eagerly awaiting the birth.

But Skylar was born with Down syndrome and a slim chance of living. Complicated surgeries repaired her esophagus. With the devoted, though tedious, efforts of family members and neighbors who took turns twenty-four hours a day manipulating the baby's arms and legs into crawling and walking positions, they programmed the baby's ability to crawl and walk. For several years Skylar and her parents struggled with her challenges. And, at six years, with her hair bouncing in adorable pigtails, Skylar attended school and often surprised her attorney parents and grandparents with her unexpected abilities.

Four years later, at ten, Skylar attends elementary school with typical third grade children. She's taken out of class for certain subjects and has a helper one-on-one with her at all times. She reads at a third grade level, swims, dances, and loves to tease. She's mastered using a computer. According to her grandmother, "She's better at it than I am. You name it, she does it. She has an unbelievable memory and never forgets anything she reads or hears. It's amazing."

Her grandmother calls her, "A real trouper with a great spirit and a wonderfully dry sense of humor," describing the way Skylar handles her continuing health issues. "I attribute all of Skylar's accomplishments to her mother's hard work and determination. No mother could be prouder of a daughter than I am," continues her grandmother. "Now I have ten grandchildren. I love them all. As for Skylar, she's the top of the Christmas tree for me. She will always be special. She is part of my heart."

Kristin is an 18-year-old high school senior with Down syndrome who became a Homecoming Queen to a joyous standing ovation from the bleachers. "Everyone stood up, crying and cheering for Kristin," said a longtime friend and fellow senior, who first met Kristin in third grade.

Increasingly, the prevalence of the Autism spectrum in children has awakened the media. The previously little-known developmental disability stole front page headlines. The recent emphasis on the frightening British statistic, one autistic child in every 80 births, proved the need for attention with stunning clarity. In the United States the recent statistic is an average of one child in every 110 births.

I was introduced to autism, to research and its treatment, through the help of my collaborator, Susan Folstein, MD.

Personable, dedicated and compassionate, Dr. Folstein recently received two Life Achievement awards for her research and contribution to the field. She willingly uses her extensive knowledge and kindheartedness to treat patients and share information with a wider audience. After several years of Dr. Folstein's generosity, sharing her knowledge and experience to benefit this book, she met Lindsay. Lindsay was having a difficult time. In short order Dr. Folstein zeroed in on the issues. The result; Lindsay is better adjusted to her daily life and far happier.

The plight of older children and adults with special needs also is fostering new support organizations, both local and national. Formerly, many died in young adulthood, but now these children are living longer. Educational programs for them end at age 22. A group including doctors, parents and other caring adults is developing a project in South Florida to fill the vacuum of "What is available for an adult with special needs after 22 years of age?" It is named Autism after 21; Life Skills for Independent Living. Its' name and sub-title describe its mission perfectly.

Betsy, a Florida teenager with autism, lives at home. She is the daughter of a divorced mother who is devoted to making Betsy's life the best it can be. She is succeeding. Betsy attends a high school with special classes. She belongs to a competitive cheerleading team and travels to competitions. She is a friendly and happy youngster, enthused about her cheerleading.

Also in Florida, an organization named Horses for the Handicapped is just what the name implies, it is a group teaching horseback riding to youngsters with disabilities. The work of this organization makes a genuine difference in these young people's lives.

In California teenagers with special needs are being taught to surf in the Pacific Ocean

"Will I Be on Television?"

Andrea, a California teacher, is soft spoken and slender with lovely long brown hair. This twenty-two year old young woman talked to me of working with developmentally disabled young people and described her students with unusual understanding. Licensed to be a teacher of young people with special needs, she spoke of how she, herself, was educated as a child in special needs classes. "I was called retarded," she said with saddened eyes. "I know how it feels." Andrea not only instructs but, borne of her own experience, she has a deep empathy with her students and what they face.

These are just a few of the success stories that have been impressive during the past six years. Perhaps your child is not the child you'd hoped for, nor the one you'd expected. Nevertheless, the doctor was right who said, "A family with a Special Needs child has something special." Sam's grandfather was right when he said, "This defines love." Skylar's grandmother was right, saying with her own love of a granddaughter, "She is the top of the Christmas tree for me."

We are right when our heart makes room for the real person inside our own child or a relative's child or the neighbor's down the block or an adult who works in a store that serves the public.

A father's story of his son. At a fundraising dinner for a school that serves children with learning disabilities, the father of one of the students delivered a speech that never would be forgotten by all who attended.

After extolling the school and its dedicated staff, he offered a question: "When not interfered with by outside influences everything nature does is done to perfection. Yet my son Shay, cannot learn things as other children do. He cannot understand things as other children do. Where is the natural order of things in my son?"

The father continued, "I believe that when a child like Shay, who was mentally and physically disabled comes into the world, an opportunity to realize true human nature presents itself, and it comes in the way other people treat that child." Then he told the following story:

"Shay and I walked past a park where some boys Shay knew were playing baseball. Shay asked, 'Do you think they'll let me play?' I knew that most of the boys would not want someone like Shay on their team, but as a father I also understood that if my son were allowed to play, it would give him a much needed sense of belonging and some confidence to be accepted by others in spite of his handicaps.

"I approached one of the boys on the field and asked (not expecting much) if Shay could play. The boy looked around for guidance and said, 'We're losing by six runs and the game is in the eighth inning. I guess he can be on our team and we'll try to put him in to bat in the ninth inning. Shay struggled over to the team's bench and, with a broad smile, put on a team shirt. I watched with a small tear in my eye and warmth in my heart. The boys saw my joy at my son being accepted.

"In the bottom of the eighth inning, Shay's team scored a few runs but was still behind by three. In the top of the ninth inning, Shay put on a glove and played in the right field. Even though no hits came his way, he was obviously ecstatic just to be in the game and on the field, grinning from ear to ear as I waved to him from the stands. In the bottom of the ninth inning, Shay's team scored again.

"Now, with two outs and the bases loaded, the potential winning run was on base and Shay was scheduled to be the next at bat. At this juncture, do they let Shay bat and give away their chance to win the game?

"Surprisingly, Shay was given the bat. Everyone knew that a hit was all but impossible because Shay didn't even know to hold the bat properly, much less connect with the ball.

"Will I Be on Television?"

"However, as Shay stepped up to the plate, the pitcher, recognizing that the other team was putting aside winning aside for this moment in Shay's life, moved in a few steps to lob the ball in softly so Shay could at least make contact.

"The first pitch came and Shay swing clumsily and missed. The pitcher again took a few steps forward to toss the ball softly toward Shay. As the pitch came in, Shay swung at the ball and hit a slow ground ball right back to the pitcher. The game would now be over.

"The pitcher picked up the soft grounder and could have easily thrown the ball to the first baseman. Shay would have been out and that would have been the end of the game....Instead, the pitcher threw the ball right over the first baseman's head, out of reach of all team mates. Everyone from the stands and both teams started yelling, 'Shay, run to first! Run to first!'

"Never in his life had Shay run that far, but he made it to first base. He scampered down the baseline, wide-eyed and startled. Everyone yelled, 'Run to second, run to second!' Catching his breath, Shay awkwardly ran toward second base, gleaming and struggling to make it to the base. By the time Shay rounded toward second base, the right fielder had the ball. He was the smallest guy on the other team. He now had his first chance to be the hero for his team.

"He could have thrown the ball to the second baseman for the tag, but he understood the pitcher's intentions so he, too, intentionally threw the ball high and far over the third baseman's head. Shay ran toward third base deliriously as the runners ahead of him circled the bases toward home. All were screaming, Shay, Shay, All the Way Shay!'

"Shay reached third base because the opposing shortstop ran to help him by turning him in the direction of third base. He shouted, 'Run to third! Shay, run to third! As Shay rounded third, the boys from both teams and the spectators were on their feet screaming, 'Shay, run home! Run home!'

"Shay ran to home, stepped on the plate and was cheered as the hero who hit the grand slam and won the game for his team. "That day," said the father softly, tears now rolling down his face, "the boys from both teams helped bring a piece of true love and humanity into this world.

"Shay didn't make it to another summer. He died that winter, having never forgotten being the hero and making me so happy coming home and seeing his mother tearfully embrace her little hero of the day."

Permission

The story of Shay is from the Maggid series of books by Rabbi Paysach J. Krohn. It is reprinted with the permission of the author and the publisher.

Afterword

Your Journey will begin where mine began, by reaching out. It took years of research to find the resources available today.

Finding Services for Special Needs Children
By Susan E. Folstein, M.D

Diagnosis and early intervention

When you, as a parent, first suspect that something is amiss—poor social interaction, slow motor development, language not developing or developing abnormally—it can be difficult to convince your primary care provider to refer you for evaluation. Early milestones are achieved at variable rates and your primary care physician (PCP) sees many worried parents whose children go on to develop normally. However, mothers are often right about their children, especially about socialization and language development, so you need to insist upon a referral.

There are several options and no one is really better than the other in terms of a place to start. If motor development is abnormal or if the child has epileptic seizures, it is best to start by seeing a neurologist but otherwise, a developmental pediatrician or developmental psychologist is a good starting place.

At this stage you have two goals. First, get a diagnosis if possible. It may not be possible to be sure in a very young child just what the diagnosis is. Don't be too concerned about this. Even more important is to start getting treatment for the aspect of development that is amiss: speech therapy and physical therapy are often useful. Behavior therapy can be important if the child is having tantrums or their behavior is otherwise unmanageable.

Many children with developmental problems have challenging behaviors. It is important for you as a parent to learn how to manage them. Some parents think that if they send their child to therapy that is going to solve the problems, but you have to continue the work at home and use methods that are the same as those used by the therapist. For many children you have to learn to be a super-consistent super –active parent. You also need to be involved in speech therapy.

Most communities have something called "early intervention" or "child find" that can do some of the diagnostic work and organize the appropriate treatments.

Very soon in the process, you need to get genetic testing. We now know many genes that cause or predispose to intellectual disability (ID) and autism spectrum disorder (ASD). Some of these can be passed on to your other children. Find a pediatrician (MD) geneticist who is expert in syndrome identification. (Some, but not most, pediatric neurologists are trained in this also.) The evaluation will include a detailed physical examination to look for abnormal physical features, blood work to send off for gene identification, and perhaps an MRI or EEG.

School

The early intervention program will advise you about what type of school is appropriate and when to start; it may start as early as 2 years old. There are several reasons for early schooling: speech therapy and behavior therapy for maladaptive behaviors can take place there and it is an opportunity for beginning to learn social skills. Also, if your child's behavior is extremely challenging, it gives you a few hours each day to be with your other children or to go to the grocery store.

If your child's problems are less severe, or if you are in denial that they exist, the problems may only be detected when he/she starts school, usually at age 4 in pre-kindergarten, Pre-K4. Mild ID or ASD may only be detected when a child needs to socialize, follow rules, or learn the alphabet. Such a child may or may not be manageable in a regular classroom, depending on many variables: can the teacher get the child to learn to follow rules, such as sitting quietly and listening? Is the child's cognitive level up to the expectations of a Pre-Kindergarten to Grade 4 classroom?

If not, your quest to find the right educational setting begins. There are many variables that go into making this decision: do the public schools in your area have good programs for children with ID or ASD, are there classes with children at a similar level to yours, do you want to try to keep your child in a regular classroom with an aid, can you afford a private school and are the ones in your area any better than the public schools? The decisions depend on where you live and cannot be considered in detail here. You will need to get in touch with other parents (Parent-to-Parent, Association for Retarded Children (ARC), etc). You may wish to hire a consultant.

The next step is to work with the school to develop an Individual Educational Plan (IEP). This requires that the school test your child first to decide what services are needed; there is often a long delay if the school system is under-funded as many are. You need to push for this, but too much pushing can result in an adversarial relationship with the school which is also counterproductive. Usually you will think that your child needs more services than the school is willing to offer, so be careful with your priorities. Some parents hire an advocate to help them with this process if it does not go well.

Often you do not make the right school choice the first time. For example, mainstreaming is not a panacea: sometimes the social demands make the child so anxious that he/she cannot perform or begins to rebel, sometimes the child is bullied, sometimes the child makes such awkward social approaches to the other children that they avoid the child. Other children do well. In general, I find that parents aim for too high achievement at first. This is understandable because we always hope for the best with our children, but you must figure out whether your child is capable of learning at the level of his classroom and whether he is being properly taught. Sometimes, it is useful to get educational or neuropsychological testing independent of the school system.

Other difficult choices and challenges come with transition to middle school and high school. Again, you may not make the right decision the first time.

Psychiatric care

Children with below average intelligence, or with ASD at whatever IQ, have high rates of psychiatric disorders that need to be treated if your child is to work to his full potential academically and socially. Common problems are ADHD, anxiety, depression, and after puberty, bipolar disorder. There can also be problems related to social relationships. Adolescents want to have boyfriends or girlfriends and be on Facebook but do not have the social judgment to appreciate the dangers this involves for someone with little or no social judgment.

It can be difficult to find a psychiatrist who is willing to care for people with ID or ASD. If you live near a university with a medical school, a good place to start is the division of child and adolescent psychiatry. Groups like Parent-to-Parent and CARD often have names of psychiatrists who they have found helpful.

Medical care

Similarly it can be hard to find pediatricians, dentists, and medical specialists who are willing to care for your child. Again, try the university and local advocacy groups.

Transition from high school to college or work

Children with developmental disorders are mandated to have a free education until either age 21 or 22, depending on their state's laws. After this, services and choices are few, unless you have a lot of money. However, this is starting to change, mostly at the instance of parents who are working together or with advocacy groups to develop appropriate college programs, work training program, supported (and unsupported) jobs, and alternative living situations. You need to do your own research on the local possibilities.

The federal government provides Vocational Rehabilitation services and day programs are available through Medicaid through the Medicaid Waiver.

It may be more difficult for highly intelligent ASD persons to find work than it is for less able young adults. Sometimes they are willing to do only one specific thing that may not be available or appropriate. Almost always they interview very poorly and need an advocate to obtain employment that they can actually do quite well once hired.

Resources for Information and Help
By Jan Amis Jessup

Parents and families will appreciate the benefits of technology. A time-saving place to research your necessary information is a computer, tablet, or cell phone. The Internet may become a best friend. If the equipment is unavailable, or if you are not computer-knowledgeable, seek your local public library, where computers will be available. Most librarians will be glad to help.

It is important that the health information on website be correct and current, including recent research or news. The date information was updated or reviewed should be easy to find and often is listed at the bottom of the page.

The Web site should include information about the organization responsible for the information and those who review the health information before it is posted. If the site has advertisements, these should be separate from the health information. It is important to review linked sites, as well.

Using your device, go to the Internet screen. Google, Yahoo and Bing are search engines. Type key words in the search box at the top of the screen. The Google search box is quick and easy. Type in words such as Autism, Down syndrome, SIDS or one of the Web sites listed below.

A Web site's address, called a "URL" gives you some of this information. The final letters in the address denote the organization that owns or sponsors the site.

.gov—The U.S. federal government
.edu –A public or private school
.org—A non-profit organization
.com-A business

"Will I Be on Television?"

MayoClinic.org is a good place to start. As an example, enter Autism in the search bar, usually found at the top of the page. You will find a list of links that will take you to Definition, Symptoms, Tests you may have.

In the search bar of your favorite Web site, or Google, enter the words that express exactly what you are searching, such as: Diagnosis of Mental Retardation, Early Intervention for a (or my) Child with Special Needs, Autism, Down syndrome, Sudden Infant Death Prevention, Attention deficit disorder (ADD), Attention deficit hyperactivity disorder (ADHD), Auditory Neuropathy Spectrum Disorder (ANSD). Also, you can enter Diagnosis of —-, Symptoms of —-, or Tests. All following Web sites have been carefully researched.

Medical

You also will find General Information on many of these sites:

CDC Centers for Disease Control and Prevention
www.cdc.gov

American Academy of Pediatrics, Articles regarding Special Needs
www.aap.org

MedlinePlus
www.medlineplus.gov
Follow the link for children and teenagers

Healthfinder
www.healthfinder.gov

National Institute of Child Health & Human Development
www.nichd.nih.gov
In the site's search box type in Special Needs

National Dissemination Center for Children with Disabilities
www.nichy.org

National Institute of Mental Health
www.nimh.nih.gov/
In the site's search box type in Special Needs

The Waisman Center, University of Wisconsin, Madison
www.Waisman.Wisc.edu

Shriners Hospitals for Children
www.shrinershospitalsforchilren.org

Nemours. A Children's Health System
www.nemours.org/

The Autism Society of America
www.autism-society.org

Autism Research Institute
www.autism.com

CDC Autism Information Center
www.cdc.gov This site provides valuable information on autism, Down syndrome, and ADHD

Autism Organizations | Autism Key
www.autismkey.com/autism-organizations/

Down Syndrome Research Center
www.dsrtf.org

Sanford School of Medicine, Down Syndrome Research Center
http://dsresearch.standford.edu

For Preventing Sudden Infant Death Syndrome, American Lung Association
www.lung.org

The CJ Foundation for SIDS
www.cjsids.org

Support Organizations

Support Organizations for specific developmental disorders can be excellent resources for information and help. Information from your state offices can direct you to the local groups of national organizations.

American Association on Intellectual and Developmental Disabilities
www.aaidd.org

United Health Care Children's Foundation
www.uhc.com

The National Association of State Directors of Development Disabilities Services, NASDDDS
www.nasddds.org/

Military OneSource
www.militaryonesource.mil

The Arc for People with Intellectual and Developmental Disabilities
www.thearc.org/

Parent to Parent USA
www.p2pusa.org

CARD Center for Autism and Related Disorders
www.centerforautism.com/

National Autism Association
www.nationalautismassociation.org/

Autism Key, Support for the Autism Community Since 2005
www.autismkey.com/autism-organizations/

The Autism Society of America—Information and Referral Center
www.autism-society.org –Select Information and Referral Center

Autism Speaks
www.autismspeaks.org

The Autism Society of America
www.autism-society.org

Kennedy Krieger Institute
www.kennedykrieger.org

Dan Marino Foundation
www.danmarinofoundation.org

Global Down syndrome Foundation
www.globaldownsyndrome.org

National Down Syndrome Society
www.ndss.org

National Association for Down Syndrome
www.nads.org

National Buddy Walk Program
www.ndss.org/Buddy -Walk

Special Olympics
www.specialolympics.org

American Sudden Infant Death Syndrome Institute
www.sids.org/

Nemours. A Children's Health System, ADD, ADHD
www.nemours.org/

Education

States' departments of education oversee disability education for children and adults. In the box of your search engine enter Education for the Developmentally Disabled. Add your state name. Follow the links for what you seek. To locate private schools enter the words, Private Schools for Special Needs children/adults on your state's home page, or go to the government websites. Searching for state and local education resources will be helpful.

Office of Special Education and Rehabilitation Services (OSERS) ED.gov
    US Department of Education
www.ed.gov/about/offices/list/osers/osep/index.html

Tufts University, Child and Family Web Guide
www.cfw.tufts.edu

National Center on Secondary Education and Transition(NCSET)
www.ncset.org/

National Military Family Association
Search for this listing, above, with search engine (google). Choose Individual Education Program link.

I.S.E.R. Internet Special Education Resources.
Special Education & Learning Disabilities Resources: A Nationwide Directory
www.iser.com

Stewart Home School
www.stewarthome.com

Education Directory for Children with Special Needs – Military
www.onesource.mil>EFMP/Special Needs

Education for All Handicapped Children Act
en.wikipedia.org/…Education_for_All_Handicapped_Children…

EXAMPLES OF LOCAL OPPORTUNITIES

Boca Accredited Alternative School, Boca Raton, Florida
www.gonha.org

Glen Lake School, Hopkins, Minnesota
www.hopkinsschools.org/glen-lake-elementary

Mostyn Moreno Educational Foundation, Texas Gulf Coast Region
www.mostynmoreno.org

Financial

Social Security, Benefits For Children with Disabilities (Pamphlet)
www.socialsecurity.gov

National Resource Directory
www.nrd.gov

United Healthcare Children's Foundation
www.uhccf.org

Easter Seals Programs for Children
www.easterseals.com

"Will I Be on Television?"

The M.O.R.G.A.N Project
www.themorganproject.org

Aid for Autistic Children Foundation
www.aacfinc.org

Autism Support Network
www.autismsupportnetwork.com/resources

DoD Special Needs Parent Toolkit
www.militaryonesource.mil

Mark's money.org Financial Assistance to persons with Down syndrome
www.marksmoney.org

Grants for Special Needs
www.itaalk.org

Information regarding Special Needs Trusts for Developmentally Disabled
Enter the phrase above in your Google search box

Transition, Training and Employment

Regarding transition to adulthood and employment there are Web sites that can be of help. In addition to those listed below, the best way to find others is to enter Google in the address box at the top of your screen.

In the Google search box, enter exactly what you're looking for. As examples: "College and University Programs for Developmentally Disabled Adults" or "Vocational Training for …" or "Employment Opportunities for…"

The most successful searches may be state or local. Add your state or city name to your search subject. Clicking on links listed on government and national search pages also will help.

Local resources for transition programs and employment may be through word-of-mouth and contact with the Support Organizations listed above and those URLs listed below.

Social Security
www.socialsecurity.gov

Social Security – Benefits for Children and Adults with Disabilities
www.ssa.gov   Click Benefits

American Association for Intellectual and Developmental Disabilities
www.aaidd.org

National Resources Directory
www.nrd.gov

National Dissemination Center (IDEA)
www.nichy.org/

Adult Vocational Training
www.ask.com

U.S. Department of Labor
www.dol.gov/dol/topic/training/disabilitytraining.htm

The Arc for People with Intellectual and Developmental Disabilities
www.thearc.org

DisABLEDperson, Inc.
www.disabledperson.com

Best Buddies
www.bestbuddies.org

Bethesda Lutheran Communities
www.bethesdalutherancommunities.org

Opportunity Partners
http://opportunities.org

Examples of State and Local Services

Job Path NYC, for People with Developmental Disabilities
www.jobpathnyc.org

Project Genesis, Connecticut
www.projectgenesis.us/about.html

CSS Chesapeake Service Systems, Inc. Chesapeake, VA.
www.css-online.org

Opportunity Partners, Minnetonka, MN
www.opportunities.org

Woods, Pennsylvania
www.woods.org

CA.gov Employment Development Department
www.edd.ca.gov/jobs

Roi Pulse
www.residentialopportunities.org

Higher Education

University Centers for Excellence in Developmental Disabilities Education, Research & Service (AUCD—UCEDDs)
www.aucd.org

Diverse, Opening Higher Education to Students with Developmental Disabilities
www.diverseeducation.com

Lindsay shares her life in the following pictures.

"A good time in Minneapolis with family favorites. Aunt Lucille Amis, Polly Pond Holley and Me."

"Earlier years Parkwood Knolls. Betty Amis Pond and Polly."

"I had a wonderful time at Disney World"

"Minnie Mouse Hugged Me"

"Cary, Bruce and Me at Universal Studios, Orlando, Florida."

"St Coletta's School, Jefferson, Wisconsin"

"The back of our Cottage 4 Bungalow. Our Living room and bedroom windows overlook our pretty back yard."

"Another cottage in our group of homes, Victoria, Minnesota"

"The first winter at Community Living, Inc. 1974. In 2013 Community Living became one of the Bethesda Lutheran Communities."

"My special friend, Nancy Tolf, and me at our traditional Christmas Eve party. At home in Boca Raton, Florida."

"Mom, Jack and Bodie. It's Christmas in Florida."

"Roxy Heyse, my special friend who lives in Milwaukee, Wisconsin. Roxy vacations in Beaver Creek, Colorado. There, with her daughter, Roxanne, their friend Christine Moore, and Mom."

"Jan McArt is a very special friend of mine. We get together whenever I'm in Florida. She is very famous as the First Lady of Theater."

"This is Angie Feneis at my Annual Meeting.
She's been Program Director since the 70's.
Mom calls her My Special Angel."

"We like Mike Casey. He's our House Parent"

"This is Jessica, one of my house mates."

"A most sincere thank you to Susan Folstein, M.D. for her contribution to this book. She is Twice a Life Achievement Award recipient for her work in autism and genetics."

"This is me at work. I work every weekday at Opportunity Partners, Minnetonka, Minnesota."

"The first home of Opportunity Partners. founded by Volunteers 61 years ago."

"The front entrance to Opportunity Partners, 2014."

"This the rear entrance to Opportunity Partners. Our van from home drops us off here in the morning."

"Cary and I had Glamour pictures made for Mom.
This is Cary."

"This is my Glamour picture."

"This is my bedroom. My awards from OP are on my bulletin board. The cup on the bed is my award for Employee of the Month at the Wyndam Hotel."

"This is my Annual Meeting with the staff from home and work."

"My award from Opportunity Partners."

"My surprise birthday party in Florida. I REALLY was surprised!! Cary, Alice and Marcy, who came all the way from Kentucky, surprised me at the door."

"I'm blowing out my birthday cake candles and making a wish."

"Cary, Bruce, Mom and Me after my birthday party"

"I'm Queen for a Day."